baby
PRODIGY
®

baby PRODIGY®

A Guide to Raising

a Smarter, Happier Baby

Barbara Candiano-Marcus

BALLANTINE BOOKS · NEW YORK

The anecdotes in this book are not necessarily based upon the experiences of individuals. A few of the portraits are composites, and in most cases, names and identifying characteristics have been changed to protect the privacy of individuals.

No book can replace the diagnostic expertise and medical advice of a trusted physician. Please be certain to consult with your doctor before making any decisions that affect your, or your baby's, health, particularly if you suffer from any medical condition or have any symptom that may require treatment.

A Ballantine Books Trade Paperback Original

Published in the United States by Ballantine Books, an imprint of The Random House Publishing Group, a divison of Random House, Inc., New York.

Ballantine and colophon are registered trademarks of Random House, Inc.

Library of Congress Cataloging-in-Publication Data
Candiano-Marcus, Barbara.
Baby prodigy : a guide to raising a smarter, happier baby / Barbara Candiano-Marcus
p.   cm.
Includes bibliographical references.
ISBN 0-345-47765-0
1. Infants—Development. 2. Infants—Intelligence levels.
3. Cognition in infants. 4. Parent and infant. I. Title.
HQ774.C34 2005
155.42'2—dc22
2004062798

Printed in the United States of America

Ballantine Books website address: www.ballantinebooks.com

2   4   6   8   9   7   5   3   1

First Edititon

Book design by Lisa Sloane

Dedication

For my father Anthony, who passed on well before his years and will always be in my thoughts and memories. Thank you for giving me your strength and confidence.

For my mother Muriel, the best mom in the world, who taught me everything I know about how to raise my two little girls.

For my two beautiful little girls, Samantha and Lara, who inspired me to write this book and continue to inspire me every day of my life.

For everyone else in our family, thank you for your love and support.

Finally, for my husband, Richard, thank you for believing in me and for always standing beside me. Thank you for sharing your life with me and helping me raise two happy little girls. And thank you for all your help with this book. I love you very much.

Acknowledgments

One thing that I've learned in the last year is that writing a book is a collaborative effort. It is an honor and a pleasure to thank the following people for all of their help.

First, thank you Jill Stern, for just about everything. Your creative contributions, expressions, and ideas have helped to make this book more than I ever could have made it alone. I would also like to thank your husband Dave and your two children Maddy and Caleb.

I am similarly indebted to Allison Dickens, the best editor a writer could wish for and one of the nicest people I know and to her editorial assistant, Ingrid Powell. Thank you both for all of your hard work.

Anthony Ziccardi, my good friend, you had the foresight to believe in me. If one person could take the credit for making this project a reality, it would have to be you. With all of my heart and soul, I thank you for giving me the opportunity of a lifetime.

Nancy Miller, my editor in chief, the Captain of my Ship, thank you, too, for believing in me.

Shona McCarthy, Alexandra Krijgsman, Benjamin Dreyer, and Lisa Feuer, the behind-the-scenes people, thank you for your tireless work on this project.

The credit for the fantastic cover of this book is owed solely to Derek Walls and Gene Mydlowski. Thank you both for a job well done.

To Jesseca Salky (publicity and marketing), thank you for helping to make Dookie & Dottie household names.

Thank you, Nora Korn, my dear friend whom I've known forever.

Besides these wonderful people who helped to make this book a reality, I am equally indebted to the people who exceeded all of my expectations in their work product. First on the list is Roger Carpenter. Thank you for designing my first video cover, which helped tremendously in getting the ball to roll.

Thank you, Tom Estey, the best publicist in the world, for all of your help.

Greg Williams and Steve Sherman, thank you for bringing Dookie and Dottie to life.

Tony Mora, thanks for all of the great illustrations and your animation.

There could, of course, be no book without a publisher. Words cannot express my gratitude to Random House and Ballantine Books for offering me the unique opportunity to share my ideas and experiences with the world.

Gina Centrello, thank you so much for the honor and privilege of working with you and Random House to publish this amazing book.

Finally, I would like to thank my husband Richard, who has been a tremendous help to me and a wonderful father to our two daughters, Samantha and Lara. I couldn't have written this book without you.

Contents

Introduction

$\mathcal{Y}$ou may not know me, but we share the same thing: We are parents who want the best for our children. That's why I started my company, the Baby Prodigy Company, and why I am writing this book. I want the best for my children and I want to help other parents, grandparents, and caregivers give their children the best.

Before my daughter Samantha was born, my husband and I, like all new parents, went out of our way to try to make sure we were prepared for her arrival. We bought a new crib, had her room decorated, and purchased tons of newborn-baby clothes and a slew of toys. We thought we were totally ready, but nothing could have prepared us for what was to come.

When the day finally arrived for us to go home from

the hospital, I excitedly took out the brand-new outfit my mother-in-law had bought especially for Samantha to wear home. We tried it on her, and to our surprise, it was way too big. I remember my husband running to the hospital gift shop searching for something—anything—that would fit our new daughter. In the end, we had to take her home in her hospital undershirt and wrapped up in two blankets.

I learned an important lesson that day, and I want to pass it on to you: Your baby doesn't need expensive outfits or fancy toys to be happy and stimulated. What she does need is something very ordinary: your love and attention. So save your energy and money and don't shop for what you *think* your baby needs.

In the chapters ahead, I share with you the practical techniques that will allow you to provide your baby with exactly what she needs to be smarter and happier. And by the way, when I packed my bag to go to the hospital and have my second daughter, I brought a simple cotton onesie, size newborn, purchased at a local superstore. It fit like a charm, and for the first few months of her life, our second daughter, Lara, wore mostly those wonderful, practical onesies.

Upon arriving home with Samantha, my husband and I settled in to adjusting to being new parents. Unfortunately, both our families lived 3,000 miles away. In the first few weeks, before anyone came to visit us, we had no extra help, only each other. I have to admit: I was completely unprepared.

I hadn't read that much about what to expect in the

first few months of a baby's life. I didn't realize how tired I would be, hadn't thought about what waking up three or four times a night to feed and change Samantha would do to my sleep cycle. After the first week at home, my husband and I were so tired we could barely keep our eyes open during the day.

Samantha was a fussy baby. She cried all the time, and all she wanted was to be held. Even if she fell asleep in my arms, the moment I tried to put her down in her bassinet, she opened her eyes and began to wail. She seemed to be so calm and relaxed when she was being held, so we cuddled her and passed her back and forth, taking turns holding her. But my efforts to keep Samantha from crying took their toll. I had no time for myself. My confidence was low, I was tired, and I was hardly enjoying being a parent. In fact, every time Samantha cried, I thought it was because I was doing something wrong.

By the time four weeks had passed, we all were starting to feel better. Samantha had settled in, and we were establishing a routine. I thought I was finally getting the hang of motherhood. And then Samantha developed colic. I didn't even know what colic was until we had endured numerous trips to our pediatrician, trying to find out what was wrong with our new daughter. All I knew was that my baby would cry and cry—no matter what I did. I was right back to thinking it was all my fault.

I did notice, however, that her crying now sounded different from when she was first born. The cries were high-pitched, like she was in pain. And there was a pattern to her crying: It lasted for hours, from six p.m. until ten p.m.

nonstop, every night. When her pediatrician told me it was colic and would probably last until she was about three months old, I was even more devastated. I didn't know how I could take two more months of her frantic crying. It got so bad that my husband and I would set the timer on the microwave at fifteen-minute intervals and take turns trying to console her. I tried everything to calm her down. Fortunately I discovered that classical music, as well as one or two baby videos that were on the market, helped to soothe Samantha and gave me a much-needed break.

After the colic stopped and I had time to get back into a routine, I decided I wanted to find a way to help other moms and dads cope with the tough times in their babies' lives. Before having Samantha I had worked in television production. Remembering what a relief it was when Samantha would settle down in front of a video or quiet herself when classical music was played, I decided to make a video for babies. I wanted it to be both entertaining and educational—a tool to help parents learn fun, stimulating ways to interact with their children.

And so I began to research the topic of how infants learn and what they are interested in. I was amazed by what I found. The Baby Prodigy CDs and DVDs are based on my research, and now I'm incorporating that research into this book. The CDs and DVDs were created using fascinating scientific findings about how babies' brains grow and develop—a process that begins well before they even enter this world.

One of the most important things I came across in my

research for my first Baby Prodigy video was how certain types of stimulation can influence your baby's happiness. I remember thinking, *Wow, how wonderful that by stimulating your baby's senses you can affect not only her intelligence but also her happiness.* What parents don't want to do everything they can to ensure their child's happiness? The most important thing to me is the happiness of my two daughters, Samantha and Lara. I know that I would do anything to help them become happy, well-rounded children. And so I decided I wanted to tell the world about this important information—about how you can help your child be happier, and smarter, too!

This book is part of my quest to spread the word. It is more than just an extension of the Baby Prodigy CDs and DVDs. It is a tool for you to use as parents or caregivers— a guide to understanding how you can stimulate your baby to make him happier and enhance his natural learning patterns.

When my second daughter, Lara, was born, I relived the stress of caring for a colicky baby, but this time I felt much more prepared. I was a much more confident, more educated mother and I found it easier to comfort Lara during those long, traumatic sessions of crying. And when she was happier, I found I was happier, too. As you read this book, remember how important it is for you as a parent, grandparent, or caregiver to be happy. During the first few months of Samantha's life, I had somehow forgotten to enjoy my baby and myself. But once I realized how important it was to take care of myself as well as my child, I became a happy mom. I firmly believe that a happy parent raises a happy child! I hope that you enjoy this book and that your kids grow up to be happy and healthy.

HOW TO USE THIS BOOK

The very first chapter discusses the scientific research that has gone into the development of my DVDs and this book. Though neurobiology research sounds as though it may be intimidating, I have tried to give you the most important information in a way that is easy to understand. I hope you will find it as fascinating as I do. If you are interested in reading more of the original scientific research, I have included a list of relevant articles and studies at the end of the book.

After chapter 1, this book is divided into sections based on the months of your baby's life, from birth until the wonderful age of two years. Chapter 2 discusses the first four weeks of your baby's life. Every moment of the relationship you and your baby share is special, but this month is unique. I talk about how the most important things you can do for your baby in her early days are to hold her, touch her, and talk to her. I also give you some suggestions of games that are gentle enough for a newborn who is adjusting to the wide world of sensory stimulation.

Chapters 3 through 8 cover months two through twenty-four, and chapter 9 offers a peek into the wild world beyond the second birthday. In each chapter, I discuss the ways in which your baby is developing, milestones she may be reaching, and how you can play with your baby to stimulate growth in the important areas of verbal skills, fine and gross motor skills, and spatial development. You will find games using common household objects, suggestions for books that are best for each age group, and ideas for toys that will be stimulating for your baby.

My goal in this book is to help you to see that every moment you spend with your baby can be an enjoyable learning experience. Other baby books are more comprehensive, talking about your post-pregnancy body and your baby's development. There is a wide variety of child-care books that are useful resources for information about a baby's feeding, sleeping, and physical well-being. I even recommend several of my trusted favorites in chapter 1. I do provide some information about your child's expected development, but mostly as background to explain some of the games I suggest you incorporate into your daily routine with your child. For an infant or child, there is no substitute for loving stimulation. You and your baby's caregivers can ensure that your baby grows up in an atmosphere conducive to being smarter and happier.

Finally, the appendix contains a list of resources, from books to websites to recommended videos and television shows.

A WORD TO CAREGIVERS

There have been many studies done that focus on the role of nonparental caregivers in infants' lives and development. These studies differentiate between the unique bonding attachment that parents and their children share and the attachment formed between a child and a nonparental caregiver. While I have always been sure, and studies now confirm, that there is no bond like that between parents and their baby, a close attachment to a caregiver plays an important role in a child's learning and development. Warm and caring relationships with adults provide children with the basis for learning. A caregiver who is sensitive to a child's unique combination of individual developmental and cultural characteristics can help that child establish self-confidence and self-worth from the earliest moments of their time together.

Whether you are reading this book as a parent who is at home full-time with your child, as a parent with a full- or part-time job, or as a caregiver who is entrusted with building a relationship with a child who is not your own, I hope you will use this book to discover new ways to view your everyday caring routines as fun-filled opportunities for learning.

A NOTE FOR PARENTS OF CHILDREN WITH SPECIAL NEEDS

No matter where your baby is developmentally, she can still benefit from your attention and positive stimulation. I have not included a separate section with specific activities for babies with special needs because many of the games and activities I suggest are appropriate and enjoyable for *any* child. Whether your baby was born prematurely and has developmental delays, has very specific needs, or has a particular diagnosis, she can still benefit from the games and activities in this book. If you find that an activity is too stimulating or challenging for your child, I recommend simply flipping back a chapter or two and trying another activity. An important part of making every moment with your child a positive learning experience is reading her cues to understand what she finds fun and interesting. And remember, all children develop differently and in many directions at once. At the same time, don't minimize something you think is important. If you have ongoing concerns about your baby's development, you should absolutely communicate them to your pediatrician.

A FINAL NOTE FOR EVERYONE

It is an awesome responsibility that is passed to you as a parent when you are handed your newborn baby. It can be overwhelming to think that you are entrusted with the physical, emotional, and mental development of the tiny creature that blinks up at you from the hospital swaddling. But there is no need to panic or feel intimidated. I want to remind you that the best way to enhance your baby's happiness and intelligence is through the attention and stimulation you provide in simple, common, day-to-day caretaking and rituals. Every day is full of experiences that stimulate and teach your baby, both directly and indirectly. I hope that this book helps you to recognize the many opportunities that await you and your baby and provides you with ideas for hours of enjoyable interactions.

baby
PRODIGY®

chapter one

Happier, Smarter Babies

As I began to research childhood brain development in order to develop the Baby Prodigy DVDs, CDs, and videos, I had to educate myself on how the brain worked. This chapter is by no means an effort to provide you with a full education in neuroanatomy; it is a simple overview of the biology and development of the brain, with an emphasis on the areas that are developing most rapidly during your child's first years of life. It's my goal to make this chapter on the science of the brain as basic and nonintimidating as possible. If, after reading this introductory material, you are as fascinated by the workings of the brain as I am, you may want to read more deeply on this subject. In the appendix, Recommended Reading and Resources, I suggest some works that explore in detail the subject of your child's developing brain.

When reading this chapter you may be surprised—as I was when I began my research in this area—by the discovery that many of the stimulating activities that promote brain growth and development in your baby are activities that we, as parents and caregivers, practice *naturally and instinctively*. In 1996, the Families and Work Institute held a conference at the University of Chicago entitled "Brain Developments in Young Children: New Frontiers for Research, Policy, and Practice." Experts from the fields of neuroscience, medicine, education, human services, media, business, and public policy discussed what was known about the developing brain and how that knowledge should inform efforts to improve results for children and their families. Their top recommendations have been distilled into a list of ten important guidelines for promoting healthy brain development in children:

1. Be warm, loving, and responsive.
2. Respond to your child's cues and clues.
3. Talk, read, and sing to your child.
4. Establish rituals and routines.
5. Encourage safe explorations and play.
6. Make television watching selective.
7. Teach through discipline. Be consistent and loving. Supervise and set limits.
8. Recognize that your child is unique and expect him to succeed.

9. Choose quality child care and stay involved.
10. Take care of yourself.

Later in this chapter I talk briefly about how each of these guidelines affects how your child's brain becomes "wired." I touch on how relationships with parents and caregivers—as well as the sights, sounds, smells, tastes, textures, and feelings children experience—help to develop the structure of the brain and shape the way your child thinks, learns, and behaves for the rest of his life. But first, a short introduction to the most important and complex structure in your body: your brain.

AN OVERVIEW OF THE BRAIN

The fully formed adult brain is a three-pound mass that allows us to think, move, feel, see, hear, taste, and smell. It controls our bodies, receives and analyzes information, and stores our memories.

Approximately 100 hundred billion long, wiry nerve cells, or neurons, send and receive electrochemical signals to and from the brain and the nervous system. The glial (meaning "glue") cells are even more numerous and act as a support system for the neurons.

The brain itself is covered by a tough coating called the dura and floats in a cushion of cerebrospinal fluid, surrounded and protected by the hard bones of your skull. The brain and the spinal cord make up the central nervous system. The brain consists of roughly four parts:

THE CEREBRUM

Also known as the frontal lobe, this intricate, wrinkled part of the brain, along with its covering, the cortex, is responsible for complex processing and high-level functions, including the following:

* behavior
* abstract thinking
* problem solving
* attention
* creative thought
* emotion
* intellect
* reflection
* judgment
* initiative
* inhibition
* coordination of movements
* eye movement
* sense of smell
* muscle movement
* physical reactions
* motor skills

The cerebrum itself has an extremely complicated structure, containing the right and left hemispheres of the brain; the occipital, parietal, and temporal lobes; and the corpus callosum.

* **The right and left hemispheres.** Control many physical and mental functions. The right side of your brain controls the left side of your body, and the left side of your brain controls the right side of your body! The right hemisphere governs temporal and spatial relationships; analyzes nonverbal information such as pattern recognition, line orientation, and complex auditory tones; and communicates emotion. The left hemisphere works to produce and understand language and controls other cognitive functions. In most people, the left hemisphere of the brain is dominant over the right in deciding what response to make.

* **The occipital lobe.** Controls vision and reading.

* **The parietal lobe.** Has some visual, language, and reading functions, but primarily governs sensory combinations and comprehension of stimuli. Your sense of touch is dependent on your parietal lobe.

* **The temporal lobe.** Also pitches in on visual and language duties, but is more strongly associated with hearing, auditory and visual memory, music, behavior, and emotion, including strong emotions such as fear. The temporal lobe plays an important role in an individual's sense of identity.

* **The corpus callosum.** Keeps communication flowing between the left and right sides of the brain.

The Brain Stem

Sometimes called the lower brain, this section controls motor and sensory pathways to the body and face, and governs vital centers of the body, including the cardiac, respiratory, and vasomotor centers.

The Cerebellum

Located just above the brain stem, the cerebellum also governs the cardiac, respiratory, and vasomotor centers. It also coordinates your sense of balance and muscle movement.

The Limbic System

Finally, the limbic system lies above the brain stem and under the cortex. It consists of a number of interconnected structures that researchers have linked to hormones, drives, aggressive behavior, strong emotions and the physiological changes that accompany them, temperature control, and memory formation.

HOW YOUR BABY'S BRAIN DEVELOPS

Your baby's brain begins forming just three weeks after conception and continues its development over a lifetime. While genetics do predispose us to develop in certain ways, researchers have found that parents and caregivers have the ability to influence brain growth in awesome ways. Proper stimulation will make your baby's brain grow denser, quicken his thought processes, and enhance his perceptive capabilities. With the right brain stimulation, experts tell us, your child will be smarter, more competent— even happier.

Babies are born with 100 billion neurons—roughly the same number they'll always have. Although they come into the world with all the neurons they need, and then some, the architecture of a baby's brain is far from developed. Over the next three years, until a baby's brain reaches nearly 90 percent of its adult size, trillions of connections— called synapses—are formed between neurons. Synapses act as bridges, establishing the brain's circuitry. The higher the quality of the synaptic connection, the quicker the brain can process information.

By the age of three, your child will have developed an estimated 1,000 trillion synaptic connections. The type and quality of these synaptic connections are determined by the kind of stimulation a baby receives from her world. The more a synapse is used in daily life, the more it is reinforced. A synapse that is not used often enough is eventually pruned away. Or, as neuroscientists like to say, "cells that fire together wire together."

My favorite analogy to illustrate how synapses are strengthened or discarded over time compares them to the trails created by travelers who are making their way through a previously uncharted wilderness. Footpaths that are frequently traveled soon become easily accessed and eventually become roadways that allow travelers to move quickly and efficiently. Other paths, which started out as equally possible routes but which are not traveled frequently, soon become overgrown, unused, and finally impassable.

In the first three years of brain development, production of synaptic connections far outpaces elimination. By the age of three, your child's brain has nearly twice the number of synapses as yours. For the rest of her first decade, production and elimination of synapses are virtually equal. Beginning in early adolescence and continuing for the rest of her life, elimination of discarded synapses becomes the dominant process. Researchers use the term "plasticity" to describe this creating, strengthening, and discarding of synapses and neuronal pathways in response to the environment. Essentially, because the brain develops in an adaptive way, it will adapt to both positive and negative environments.

So what does this mean for *your* baby? In a nutshell: For the first three years of her life, the stimulation she receives and the experiences she has will influence how her brain will be wired as an adult.

BABIES ARE LEARNING MACHINES

From the moment your baby is born, he is interacting with his environment. And these interactions will shape the development of his brain as he grows. Babies who receive warm, responsive care from the beginning of their lives are more likely to thrive and to show more resilience later in life than those who receive lesser care. On the most basic level, we know that good care facilitates good brain development.

Your baby is a learning machine. Everything is interesting to him. So how can you have the most enriching impact on your child's brain development?

At birth, the lower brain largely controls your newborn's behavior. All of her reflex motions, even her cycles of crying and sleeping, are functions of the brain stem and the spinal cord. The rest of her brain—the cerebrum, cerebellum, and limbic system—develops at a more leisurely pace, which gives you an opportunity to enhance your baby's environment and experience to shape her developing mind.

You'll be encouraged to know that you don't need fancy gizmos to help your baby reach her full potential. *You* are your child's greatest tool for learning, enjoyment, and development. A smarter, happier baby is one who receives normal, loving, responsive care that provides her with many opportunities to experience the sights, sounds, smells, textures, and emotions of everyday life. The stimulation provided by this interaction with you and her environment will strengthen the structure of her brain. One form of stimulation that has been proven to be of significant benefit is language. Language is fundamental to cognitive development, and the simple act of talking—and listening—to your child is one of the best brain-building exercises I can recommend.

PUTTING SCIENCE INTO PRACTICE

In the chapters that follow, I offer you concrete ideas for practicing the kind of care and creating the kind of environment that will allow your child to thrive. I encourage you to take a conscious approach to promoting your child's happiness and confidence. In doing so, you'll raise a smarter child. Before you turn to the next chapter and start looking at specific suggestions, I want to briefly return to the ten guidelines for promoting brain development that I mentioned at the beginning of the chapter. Whether your child is one month old or two years old, there are ways to promote her growth by paying attention to each of these areas in your daily care routines.

1. **Be warm, loving, and responsive.** Cuddling, rocking, and letting your child focus on your loving expression helps her to create memories, which in turn will allow for a smooth flow of information as she learns to access them efficiently. Secure attachments are the basis of all of your child's future relationships.

2. **Respond to your child's cues and clues.** Learn to read your infant's nonverbal signals and understand his cries. Translate your toddler's early attempts at language. Become familiar with his facial expressions and body language. Responding quickly and appropriately builds trust and reduces stress. A secure child is more likely to be curious and open to new experiences and stimulation.

3. **Talk, read, and sing to your child.** Repetition is important in both building language skills and understanding speech. The more you talk to your child, the more the language-sensitive parts of his

brain will grow. Reading and singing to your child foster anticipation and participation.

4. **Establish rituals and routines.** Repeated positive experiences help neurons form strong connections that help a child learn what to expect and how to react. Daily rituals and routines strengthen the creation of memories that will be accessed in increasingly complicated ways.

5. **Encourage safe explorations and play.** Encourage your baby or toddler to explore his world. Sensory input is valuable stimulation, and children learn through play.

6. **Make television watching selective.** Watch television with your child and talk about what you are seeing. Educational programming is enhanced when it is an interactive event.

7. **Teach through discipline. Be consistent and loving. Supervise and set limits.** Teaching your child self-control takes time, as this is governed by one of the more slowly developing parts of the brain. Never hit or shake a child. Brain research shows that such treatment can have long-term negative effects.

8. **Recognize that your child is unique and expect him to succeed.** Children have different growth rates, both mentally and physically. Work with your child's temperament to help him see the connections between his actions and your response. Encourage positive self-esteem.

9. **Choose quality child care and stay involved.** Be

sure that any caregiver involved in your child's life responds quickly and warmly to your child's needs.

10. **Take care of yourself.** The responsibility of child rearing is daunting, and providing your child with quality stimulation can sometimes be challenging and occasionally overwhelming. Ask for help if you need it. Rest and recharge as needed, and never feel guilty. You are doing important work.

If you want to read more about current research and thinking in the field of neuroscience and children, I have listed a number of fascinating books and articles in the appendix.

You're ready to get to work—and you have been all along. Raising a happier, smarter baby is no more difficult than enjoying each day you spend interacting with your own wonderful, amazing child. I hope you're inspired by the chapters that follow and that you'll engage with your child with the full understanding of how science and caregiving come together to allow your child to reach his full and rich potential.

chapter two

Getting to Know You: Birth through Four Weeks

When our second daughter, Lara, was born, I felt a lot more confident taking her home from the hospital than I did when we brought our first daughter, Samantha, home. Although I realized we now had twice the work ahead of us and new obstacles to face, I still felt confident—after all, I'd already done this once! However, what I didn't do two years earlier was take care of myself and let our friends and family help while I recovered from a painful C-section and the shock of being a new mom. So when Lara came along, I vowed I would take care of myself, as well as the children. Now that our daughters are five and three, I look back and see how much easier it was for all of us the second time around. I learned that for me to be a happy person and a happy mom, I had to accept help and, more important, take care of myself!

Barbara, Samantha and Lara's mom

HOMECOMING

The day you have dreamed of is finally here: You're taking your new baby home from the hospital. In the final months of your pregnancy, you probably fantasized about this precious time—the peaceful moments you would spend rocking your baby, sipping herbal tea in the spotless nursery. You may have convinced yourself that you'll quickly return to your normal schedule and life now that you and baby are finally home. I know one mother who was quite certain, after leaving the hospital on December 23, four days after a difficult Cesarean delivery, that she could still manage to finish the holiday decorating that had been interrupted by the baby's arrival, including wrapping presents for her five-year-old.

There is nothing more wonderful than coming home with the tiny baby you've been thinking about for the last nine months, but I feel compelled to warn you that if you're like most of us, over the next few hours, days, or weeks, you'll be shaken out of your beautiful daydream and you may have to alter your ambitious plans. I can definitely guarantee—whether this is your first baby or your fourth—there will be times in these early weeks when the reality of your new responsibility overwhelms you. But you don't need to panic. Many others have been exactly where you are now and survived! There are time-tested techniques that will keep you and your baby happy and connected in these early days together.

SOME IMPORTANT ADVICE FOR NEW PARENTS

To set your newborn on course to being a smarter, happier baby, there is a single piece of advice that it is imperative you follow in the first weeks. And that is to *take care of yourself.* Accept all offers of help: extra hands, prepared meals, or any other conveniences friends and family may offer. You will need all your strength, both mentally and physically, to be the best parent you can be to your newborn. For the moment, forget all of the clothing and toys and gadgets you received at your baby shower or rushed out and bought in the weeks before the baby was due. Your baby comes out of the womb with an instinct for survival, and for the next few weeks, her needs are simple and repetitive: food, clean clothes, shelter, and, most important, you. So make sure that you're able to be there for her. Simply holding your baby and spending time with her promotes bonding and a sense of security that will comfort and satisfy her. And, as the days pass, you'll gradually be able to establish the patterns of feeding and sleeping that work best for your baby and your family.

TOP THREE TIPS FOR THE FIRST FOUR WEEKS

Make sure you get enough sleep: Newborns sleep from twelve to twenty hours in a twenty-four-hour period, waking and sleeping in short intervals. Since a newborn may want to eat as often as every two hours, take advantage of your baby's sleepy periods and sneak in a nap whenever you are able.

Things You Need/Things You Don't

Despite what all the baby catalogs would have you be-lieve, the material needs of a newborn are surpris-ingly minimal. Here's a short list of what I couldn't have done without—as well as those things I can't believe I thought I would need!

Most Useful Items for a Newborn:

- **100 percent cotton onesies.** My babies lived in these for the first few weeks.

- **Cotton receiving blankets** have a multitude of uses includ-ing wiping up spit-up, keeping baby propped on his side, and swaddling.

- **A front pack or sling for carrying your baby** will be an in-vestment you never regret, especially if you have a colicky baby.

- **An infant car seat** is required for you to leave the hospital with your baby.

Make sure you get enough nourishment: It is recom-mended that women who are breast-feeding consume an extra 400 to 500 calories per day beyond the caloric intake necessary to maintain their normal (pre-pregnancy) weight. If you are bottle-feeding your baby, you still need to pay attention to your diet. Eat healthy meals and avoid ex-cess caffeine or sugary treats. Good nutrition will help you maintain your energy level.

Trust your instincts: There are many, many child-care and parenting books; I recommend several that I like later

- **A diaper bag.** You won't believe how much stuff there is to carry around for such a tiny creature!

- **A good baby-care reference book.** Invaluable for answering those nagging middle-of-the-night questions and concerns.

- **Baby wipes.** Lots and lots of baby wipes.

Least Useful Items for a Newborn:

- **A portable crib or playpen** is something you can wait to purchase. For the first month, your baby will probably be in her crib, worn in a front pack or sling, or in the arms of an adoring parent, relative, or caregiver.

- **Baby swing.** Babies under six weeks do not have strong muscle control of their heads and necks, and slumping in swings can be dangerous.

- **Fancy, frilly, scratchy outfits** may look adorable, but may not be the most comfortable against tender newborn skin.

- **Plush crib toys** can be a hazard for newborns.

in this chapter. But when it comes down to knowing what will work best for the little person who has entered your life, you must learn to trust your instincts. What is right for your sister's son or your best friend's daughter may not be right for your baby. And what worked for your first baby may not work at all for your second. When you have questions—and you will—consult the library of books from child-care experts or check in with your family, friends, or pediatrician. And after weighing all their good advice, decide what works best for you and your baby.

Bookshelf

While I'm sure you can't wait to start sharing your favorite childhood books with your
new baby, I've chosen the books listed below especially for you! A newborn baby is often overwhelming, and
even if it's not your first child, there's always a time when you
can use a little impartial reassurance. It's vital that you feel
confident and educated as you parent your new baby, and
while information from family and friends can be invaluable, I
know how important it is to have an instant resource available for those middle-of-the-night consultations.

The following books are time-tested resources and address many of the basic questions and concerns parents
have. This book list is not meant to be exhaustive. It simply
offers my opinion on some of the best resources for parents
of babies and young children. I hope you will use the recommendations below for guidance and then combine the information you read with your own instincts and the advice of
family and friends to arrive at the solutions that work best
for you and your child.

Feel free to read sections aloud to your baby as you
comb through these books. While she may not be enthralled
by the story line, at her age, it's the sound of your voice, not
the content of your speech, that matters.

- **Dr. Spock's Baby and Child Care** by Benjamin Spock, M.D.,
  and Stephen J. Parker, M.D. The acknowledged classic, offering practical advice to new parents for more than sixty
  years.
- **Pregnancy, Childbirth, and the Newborn** by Penny Simkin,
  Janet Whalley, and Ann Keppler. This complete and authoritative guide to all aspects of childbearing, from conception

to the early days of infancy, is full of well-organized and clearly presented information. The three authors have more than 100 years of combined experience in the field of childbirth. Need I say more?

- **Secrets of the Baby Whisperer** by Tracy Hogg with Melinda Blau. With advice that is reassuring and down-to-earth, *Secrets of the Baby Whisperer* suggests simple programs that can bring peace to your household and let you relax into parenting.

- **The Baby Book** by William Sears, M.D., and Martha Sears, R.N. In this encyclopedic guide, Dr. Bill Sears and Martha Sears, drawing from their experience both as medical professionals and as parents, provide authoritative, comprehensive information on virtually every aspect of infant care.

- **Touchpoints: The Essential Reference** by T. Berry Brazelton, M.D. Brazelton offers the kindly, reassuring approach of your own family physician, providing a chronological account of the basic stages of early childhood.

- **What to Expect the First Year** by Arlene Eisenberg, Heidi Murkoff, and Sandee Hathaway. A classic, with a friendly question-and-answer format, that covers everything you might want to know about your baby's first year, as well as much you never knew you would need to know!

- **Your Baby and Child: From Birth to Age Five** by Penelope Leach. Written by a psychologist and expert in child development, who is also the mother of two, this book addresses what your child is doing, how she is feeling, what she is experiencing, and how she is developing, from birth through kindergarten.

BONDING WITH BABY

You have probably heard a lot of talk about "bonding" with your newborn. Bonding is sometimes used interchangeably with the word "attachment," but from a scientific point of view the two terms have distinct meanings. According to scientists, the concept of bonding refers to the tie a parent feels toward an infant. It occurs most naturally during the first hours or days after birth, when the experience of meeting your baby cements your connection with her and you form a permanent bond with this enchanting little individual.

From a scientific point of view, which is distinctly lacking in warm and fuzzy reciprocation, however, your baby does not bond with you! Rather, an infant becomes attached to her caregivers over time. This attachment, which is as much a lifelong commitment as bonding, is based upon the shared interactions that occur over the weeks and months of early childhood.

Scientific definition aside, what you really need to know is that these first four weeks are a critical time during which your baby depends on you to provide the kind of consistent, dependable, responsive care that will allow her to become secure and confident in herself and others. So how can you promote bonding and attachment?

The most important thing you can do during these first few weeks of life is to hold and touch your baby. Don't rely on plastic baby carriers or car seats that double as infant easy chairs. Front carriers and fabric slings make it simple to keep your baby close to you all day long. My daughter

Dookie Says

"I love it when my daddy lets me lie on his chest when he's taking care of me. It's so warm, and I can hear the sound of his heart beating. It makes me feel so relaxed. I think I'll take a nap!"

A great activity to try with your baby to promote bonding and attachment is something called "kangaroo care." This concept, developed in the 1980s in an intensive-care nursery in Bogotá, Colombia, is now used for many premature babies and in neonatal intensive-care units around the world. But your baby does not have to be premature to enjoy the benefits. Modeled on the needs of baby kangaroos, who are born only partially developed and then immediately hop into their mother's warm pouch, where they continue their development for months before emerging into the world, kangaroo care means nothing more than just holding your baby (often wearing only a diaper) against your own naked skin. Drape a blanket over your baby's back to keep him warm and just sit together. You can chat with your baby, be silent and allow him to listen to the comforting sound of your heartbeat, rock in a chair, or sit perfectly still. You can even peacefully drift off for a nap together.

Samantha was the most content when she was being held and snuggled, so my husband and I would take turns wearing her in a front pack and carrying her around the house as we tended to our own daily routines. Don't worry about "spoiling" your newborn. Your baby will gradually begin to develop patterns of eating, sleeping, and quiet alertness that will allow you to establish a routine that teaches her how to spend time in an environment other than the crook of your arm.

SLEEPING AND WAKING

By the end of this first month you may begin to notice some patterns to your baby's daily needs and moods. Her feeding times may start to become more regular—every three to four hours is average—although during growth spurts she may want to eat more. She will be awake and alert for longer periods of time, but she will still sleep about sixteen out of twenty-four hours.

Some babies at this age mix up night and day—they sleep all day and wake up and expect company at night. By the age of one month, you can help your baby shift onto the schedule followed by the rest of your household by using the following techniques:

* Prolong your baby's periods of alertness during the day. I suggest several fun ways of doing this later in this chapter.

* Try limiting daytime sleeping to three- or four-hour intervals, gently waking your baby if she is intent on sleeping for more than four hours at a time during the day.

* Have your baby sleep in different places during the day and night. During the day, have him nap somewhere other than his crib or bassinet—for instance, in his stroller. Place him in his own

bedroom or crib at night, so he will come to associate his crib with a long, quiet sleep.

* Make nighttime more conducive to sleep. Darken the room, use quiet voices or whispers when your baby wakes in the night, don't turn bright lights on for changing, feeding, etc.

* Make sure your baby isn't being *over*stimulated during the day. All babies need adequate daytime rest. Babies who receive too much stimulation can easily become overtired and may be unable to settle down to sleep well at night.

THE SIX STATES OF SLEEP AND WAKEFULNESS

Your newborn baby isn't just either asleep or awake. Believe it or not, most infants cycle in and out of six states of sleep and wakefulness. Because the way each baby transitions from each state to the next and the amount of time your baby spends in any one particular state will vary, it is helpful to be able to identify your child's state of wakefulness.

Deep sleep: Your baby is very quiet and relaxed. Her breathing is rhythmic, and while she may make spontaneous movements, she rarely awakens.

Light sleep: Your baby's eyes are closed, but he makes faces and sounds and seems generally restless. Babies may pass through this state on the way to a drowsy awake state or to a state of deep sleep.

Safety Watch: Back to Sleep

Always put your baby to sleep on a firm surface on her back. Babies who are not put to sleep on their backs are at higher risk for sudden infant death syndrome (SIDS), the unexpected and sudden death of an apparently healthy infant, usually while the baby is asleep or in bed. If your baby seems uncomfortable sleeping on her back, try swaddling her snugly in a thin blanket.

Your newborn's sleeping area should also be free of loose blankets, pillows, and plush toys. Sleeping facedown on a lambskin, soft mattress, or even a quilt has been linked to suffocation deaths. One-piece sleepers can keep your baby warm on cold nights, eliminating the need for blankets or quilts. Until your baby can roll over, you should never leave her unattended on her tummy on a soft surface (even a blanket or quilt).

Since your baby will be spending all her sleeping time on her back, it is very important to remember to let her spend time on her tummy. Not only will this promote her developing muscle coordination and strength in her neck and shoulders, it will also keep her head from becoming flat as a pancake in the back! Just be sure to keep an eye on her during tummy time.

Drowsy: Your baby is awake, but appears sleepy. Her activity level varies and her eyelids droop. She may appear cross-eyed. To wake her fully, you may stimulate her by talking to her, touching her, or picking her up.

Quiet alert: Your baby will lie still, his eyes open and bright. His breathing will be regular and calm, and he will

Games Siblings Play

Unfortunately, a newborn baby may not be very interesting to an older sibling. As far as the older child is concerned, this new addition to the family is noisy and garners more than his fair share of the attention. Some older children initially want nothing to do with the new baby, and you should try to respect their feelings and not force any unwanted interactions. Don't worry, however. Even if they get off to a less than loving start, with a little time, your children will develop the special bonds that only siblings can share.

Explain to the older child that new babies are not big enough or strong enough to play the kinds of games that an older kid enjoys playing. You may want to explain that new babies require a lot of care in doing things that bigger kids can do for themselves. If your older child wants to be involved, include her in baby-care routines that are appropriate to her age. Let her hold the baby and help with diapering, dressing, or bath time; let her burp the baby or help give him his bottle. And, of course, the entertainment value of a younger sibling cannot be underestimated. Let her talk and sing to her new sibling. Teach her to be respectful of the baby's need for space. Show her how to recognize the signs that mean the baby's had enough playtime and needs to rest.

make eye contact and focus attentively on sounds. This is the best time for you to try some of the stimulation techniques I suggest in the sections below.

Active alert: Your baby is fussy and fidgety. She is af-

Your Baby's View: Swaddling

Have you ever been to a spa and enjoyed a body wrap? If so, you'll immediately understand why your baby finds swaddling so comforting. If not, I recommend that you try it! But in the meantime, imagine that you are lying in an unfamiliar environment, and you are trying to relax. It's brighter than you're used to, and maybe noisier, too. You're exhausted, but you've had so much stimulation, you're too wound up to sleep. Now imagine someone comes into the room and dims the lights, the outside sounds become muted, and warm blankets are pulled snugly around your body. You're gently wrapped, enveloped in soft fabric. Unable to twitch restlessly or wriggle around, you allow your muscles to relax. You are cocooned in comfort. Your eyes grow heavy and you fall asleep.

Voilà! You have succumbed to the calming effects of being

fected easily by hunger, fatigue, or overstimulation. Her eyes are open, but her gaze is not as clear as while in quiet alert, and she does not focus attentively.

Crying: A baby who has reached this state needs comforting. If she is not hungry, she may be overstimulated. For ideas on how to recognize and calm a baby who has had too much stimulation, see the section below on reading your baby's cues.

BABY STEPS

Whenever you compare your newborn to a list of "shoulds," it's crucial to remember that babies are individ-

swaddled. This technique can be used to soothe an overstimulated or overtired baby. Swaddling provides a sense of security that most newborns enjoy. Once your baby is a month
old, swaddling can interfere with her exploration of motor
development, and it is best to stop wrapping your baby.

To swaddle your baby, place her diagonally on a receiving
blanket with the top left corner folded down about six
inches. Pull the lower left corner over her left arm and
across her body. Tuck the corner of the blanket in under her
right side. Take the lower right corner and bring it up over
her body, tucking the tip under the piece you have just
wrapped across her. Take the top right corner of the blanket,
pull it across her right arm, and tuck the top in around her
back. She should be wrapped snugly, but not too tightly. If
your baby protests at having her hands confined, swaddle her
using the same technique, but bring the fabric under, rather
than over, her arms.

uals and follow very different timetables. I was positive my
daughter began offering me full, happy smiles when she
was just two weeks old. No matter what they say, I'm convinced it wasn't "just gas." Another mother swears her son
was completely impassive until he was almost six weeks
old. "He just didn't seem to have much of an opinion about
anything at first," she says. Now, at six months old, he is
charmingly expressive.

By the end of one month, your child should achieve
some, or all, of the milestones listed below. If you are concerned about your child's rate of development, consult your
pediatrician.

Did You Know?: Your Baby's Senses

Sight

- Your newborn baby can focus on objects at a distance of about seven to fifteen inches, roughly the distance of his mother's face when he's feeding.

- If an infant is interested in an object, she can track it along a 180-degree arc above her head.

- Newborns are attracted to objects that have a high contrast between light and dark colors, especially patterns in black and white. They also notice shiny objects.

- You may notice that your baby is sensitive to bright lights. If you dim the lights, he may open his eyes wider and focus on objects more intently.

Hearing

- Babies can hear and react to sound, even in the womb.

- Sudden or loud noises may cause him to startle.

- Your baby may also respond to voices, especially those that are higher-pitched.

- If you played particular music or talked to your baby while he was in the womb, he will be able to recognize the sound of your voice, or even a specific tune.

Within the first four weeks, your baby should be able to:

✳ lift his head briefly
✳ focus on a face

- Babies also like sounds that remind them of familiar sounds they heard while in the womb. The sound of your heartbeat may be comforting.

- Does your baby suddenly grow less fussy when he hears the dishwasher or other appliances? External sounds such as those of a dishwasher, vacuum cleaner, or washing machine may remind your baby of similar sounds in the womb. Our daughter Samantha's favorite calming sound was the blender!

Smell

- Your baby is born with a refined sense of smell. For instance, she is able to recognize the difference in smell between her mother's milk and another mother's milk.

Taste

- Your baby may react to sweet, sour, salty, and bitter.

- Babies often prefer sweet-tasting items.

Touch

- Infants enjoy being stroked, rocked, caressed, gently jiggled, or bounced.

- They are most comfortable when they are snug and warm. Most babies will not tolerate extremes of hot and cold.

Your baby may be able to:

* respond to a noise with a startle, by crying, or by becoming quiet

* track an object held directly above her face and moved slowly to one side or the other

It is possible that, by the end of four weeks, your baby may:

* smile
* vocalize by cooing (as well as by crying)

BABY TALK

Don't worry about not knowing what your baby wants—from the instant he emerges into this world, he has ways of communicating with you, but it might take you some time to understand him. By her third week at home, one couple had nicknamed their daughter "The Little Dictator" for her habit of loudly and clearly issuing her demands. The nickname, by the way, still applied by the time their daughter had turned two! Other parents, though, report that their child's miscellaneous noises and motions seem to have no pattern. Generally, however, by paying attention to what your newborn baby is saying, you can lay the groundwork for the early development of communication skills.

How Babies Communicate

Crying

Crying is your preverbal baby's way of telling you something: He's tired, hungry, cold, bored, sick, or simply needs to be held. Cries are different, and you will learn to differentiate between your baby's vocal expressions.

* **Hungry:** Your baby starts with short cries that build to a steady rhythm of wails.

* **Tired:** Exhaustion is expressed through a distinctive pattern of short wails, followed by a longer, louder cry. If left alone, this type of crying will continue until he falls asleep.

* **Bored:** Your baby may have a period of cranky fussing that starts with irritable noises and soon escalates to crying if he is left unattended.

* **Overwhelmed:** This cry is similar to a tired cry, but your baby may also turn away from you when you try to comfort him.

* **Uncomfortable:** To understand what may be bothering your baby, consider her environment. If she is too cold, she may be shivering or have goose bumps in addition to crying. If too hot, she may pant slightly and be flushed. If she has a gas pain, her cry will be piercing and sharp and come on quite suddenly with little or no preliminary fussing.

* **Colic:** If your baby has regular periods of sustained crying that occur around the same time each day, she may be suffering from colic. (See the sidebar on Colic on page 34.)

Colic

The word "colic" can strike fear into even the most experienced parents' hearts. Colic is basically sustained crying by an otherwise healthy infant that occurs at generally regular times on a generally regular basis. Pediatricians sometimes use the "rule of three" to diagnose colic. A baby has colic when he cries for longer than three hours every day for more than three days a week, and when the crying goes away when the baby is about three months old.

About 20 percent of all babies get colic, and it affects all infants equally—boys get it as often as girls; firstborns as often as later children. Although there are many theories, ranging from food allergies to immature nervous systems to the particular temperament of each child, no one knows for sure what causes colic. What *is* known is that colic is at the extreme end of normal crying behavior, and it is a harmless, though distressing (particularly for the parents), condition.

Your baby may begin to have episodes of colic around the age of three weeks. Although colic is not thought to be due to pain, a baby with colic may look uncomfortable. She may lift her head, turn red in the face, or draw her legs up to her tummy. She may refuse to eat during her colicky time or have difficulty falling and staying asleep. The important thing to remember is that babies with colic are *healthy* babies. However, if your baby seems at all ill and has sustained crying, call your pediatrician, and she can help you determine if it is illness or colic.

As the mother of not one but two colicky babies, I'm here to tell you that there is no single, simple treatment to "cure" colic. There are a number of ways to try to soothe your colicky baby, but before I tell you what they are I want you to understand the most important message for the parent of a baby who has colic: *Do not blame yourself.* You are not the cause of your baby's distress. You have done nothing wrong, and you are not a bad parent if you are unable to completely comfort your infant during these crying episodes. Having a baby with colic can be stressful for the whole household. Try to relax and remember that your baby will eventually outgrow this phase.

In addition to muttering the mantra "This too shall pass," here are some suggestions for trying to make life easier for you and your colicky baby:

- Walk or rock your baby. Try holding her in various positions.

- Put her on your shoulder and massage her back, as if you are trying to burp her.

- Place your baby on her tummy on your knees and rub her back or gently bump her up and down

- Try an infant swing or vibrating baby chair. Babies under eight weeks should not be put in an infant swing, as they cannot hold themselves upright. Some bassinets have a vibrating feature, or you can try rocking her in a cradle.

- Go for a ride. Put your baby in the car seat and take a drive. Other parents swear by the vibration and sounds of a washing machine or clothes dryer. Do not place your infant on top of any surface unless you will be standing there *the entire time.*

- Finally, if you feel like you are at the breaking point, try to get away from your baby's crying. Trade "colic shifts" with your spouse, or cash in a favor from a grandparent or friend (often a baby's cry is not as upsetting to people who are not her parents). If you must, put the baby in her

> crib where she is safe and secure, simply close the door to her room, and take five minutes for yourself.
>
> - One of my daughters would sometimes quiet down when I put on certain CDs or videos. At the very least, soothing music in the background can provide a nice contrast to the steady cries!

GAMES

Let's Talk about It

Once you can identify what your baby is "talking" about, you can begin to name the feelings she is expressing: "Oh you're crying because you are hungry. Let me feed you." "I bet that wet diaper is uncomfortable; let's change it." "You're very tired, aren't you? How about a nap?" Use your baby's name and a conversational tone as you help her to learn to associate a response with her particular request.

Cooing

As any enamored new parent will attest, sweet baby coos are the most adorable of the nonverbal communications. Your baby's mews, coos, and sighs are all precursors to verbal development. You can help lay the groundwork for future verbal skills by talking to him in the high-pitched tone he prefers, singing, playing music, and exposing him to soft sounds of many different varieties.

Did You Know?: Reading Your Baby's Cues

From the moment your baby looks up at you in the delivery room, you may have the feeling that he's trying to tell you something. And he may be. From birth, babies have the ability to communicate a wide range of needs. If you pay attention, you will soon know what your baby likes or dislikes and what he may want at any given time.

Watch your baby and see if you can observe any of the following common means of infant communication:

- **Fussing, crying:** I'm hungry; I'm tired; I'm not comfortable; Where are you? I want you now!

- **Rooting, wakefulness, sucking on hand or lip:** I'm hungry, and if you feed me now, I won't cry.

- **Heavy eyelids:** I'm sleepy.

- **Eye contact with bright alert eyes and intent stare:** Pay attention to me.

- **Vocalizing with coos or noncrying sounds:** Let's talk.

- **Looking away or breaking eye contact:** I'm tired and need a break.

GAMES

A Night at the Opera

Make dinnertime a dinner theater experience. Sing and talk to your baby while she nurses or takes her bottle. Make up silly songs about changing diapers, having a bath, and lying in her bed. You don't have to be Pavarotti for

Toy Chest

From birth through the first four to six weeks, your baby is not too interested in anything but eating, sleeping, and bonding with you. Still, what parent can't resist buying their baby a few toys? Here are some things that your baby will actually be able to enjoy in her first month:

- **A mobile:** A black-and-white or primary-colored mobile that can be safely mounted on a changing table or crib rail will provide baby with visual stimulation.

- **Black-and-white items:** Toys or pictures in high-contrast black-and-white patterns are easy for your baby to focus on. Simple faces or shapes are most interesting to very young infants.

- **CDs:** Most babies love music. Experiment to see what your child likes best. Good choices are classical music or simple, instrumental arrangements.

your baby to be enthralled. It's the tone and timbre of your voice that she will respond to—not your ability to span five octaves.

Does This Ring a Bell?

Using a plush toy with a small, soft bell inside, shake the toy on one side of your baby's head, then the other. He may turn his head or focus his eyes in the direction of the chiming sound.

- **A brightly colored ball, or a rubber or plush toy:** Move the ball slowly across your baby's range of vision to help her coordinate her eye muscles.

- **And, of course, your baby's favorite toy: You!** Move into her range of vision and let your baby study your face. Gently touch her hands to your nose, eyes, ears, and mouth as you name the body parts. (This is a game she'll love later and will eagerly participate in when she is developing language. Playing this game with such a young baby will begin to create a memory for her.) Let her clutch at your skin, hair, or clothing to experience different textures. Hold her in your arms as you sing to her or tell her a story, or simply let her snuggle close and hear your heartbeat. All the things a loving parent does naturally with her newborn are positive stimulating activities that are building blocks to the more advanced skills your child will begin to rapidly develop.

Smiling

No that's not just gas! Babies as young as four weeks old can offer you true smiles to show they are content. Smile at your baby often, and one day she will smile back!

GAMES

Mirror, Mirror on the Wall

Encourage smiles and other facial expressions by holding your baby in front of a mirror. Although she will not recognize herself until she's around fifteen months, she will enjoy studying the very different faces of an infant and an adult.

Monkey See, Monkey Do

Hold your baby close to your face. Make different faces and show emotion. Your baby should be able to mimic some of your facial expressions. Try shaping your mouth into an O or sticking out your tongue to see if she will copy you. Although responsive smiling usually begins around six weeks, try giving her some big smiles; you may be rewarded with an endearing toothless grin in return.

THE LITTLE THINGS: FINE MOTOR SKILLS

Although your new baby won't begin working on her fine motor skills for a little while yet, one of the tests she will be given at birth gives you an idea of just how quickly she can progress. This test, called the Apgar score, after Dr. Virginia Apgar, who first developed it in the 1950s, uses a numbered scale to evaluate a newborn's physical condition. The test is given within a minute of birth, and then again five minutes after birth. A score between 7 and 10 is considered "normal." A score of 6 or less indicates that the infant is in some distress. Don't immediately panic if your baby's first score is on the lower side of normal, or even slightly below normal. A traumatic birth may result in lowered scores, but your baby's second score should show marked improvement as the delivery room team stabilizes his condition.

Five factors are evaluated and scored, with the totaled scores giving your baby's Apgar score.

Strength and regularity of heart rate		Skin color (to determine lung efficiency at oxygenating blood)	
100 beats/minute	2	Pink	2
Below 100	1	Bluish extremities	1
None	0	Totally blue	0
Lung maturity		**Reflex response to irritable stimuli**	
Regular breathing	2	Crying	2
Irregular	1	Whimpering	1
None	0	Silence	0
Muscle tone and movement			
Active	2		
Moderate	1		
Limp	0		

HOW IT ALL FITS: SPATIAL DEVELOPMENT

Your baby is curious about the world around her and from birth can see well enough to be interested in objects and people at a distance of up to fifteen inches away. If you think your new baby is looking at you expectantly, she may well be. Babies will seek eye contact when they want to be stimulated. They will turn away or pull back to break contact when they need a rest. Your baby's vision will show improvement by about two months of age, and will continue to sharpen and expand its range until it has developed to 20/20 vision by about six months old. In these early weeks, your baby will like to look at human faces, round shapes, highly contrasting light and dark colors (particularly black and white), and slowly moving objects (particularly shiny ones).

Safety Watch: A Word about Monitors

I can sympathize with every new parent who cannot resist the temptation to sneak into his baby's room and rest a hand on his infant's back—just to make sure she's breathing. One mother confessed that she would check on her daughter once or twice a night up until she was one year old. The natural instinct of any parent to protect his or her child is so strong that it's hard to blame anyone for wanting to monitor the baby during every minute of every day.

There are a wide variety of baby monitors available to help ease any worries you may have about your baby while you're not right in the room with him. There are monitors with cameras that link to video screens elsewhere in the house, providing a video image that corresponds with the various grunts, squeaks, and snorts that a newborn infant makes day and night. There are simple monitors that allow you to hear sound only.

There are even monitors designed to attach to your infant with thin wires to let you know how she is breathing.

GAMES

Follow the Bouncing Ball

Using a brightly colored rubber or plush ball about two inches in diameter, hold the ball about twelve to fifteen inches above your baby's head and slowly move it up and down, side to side, in and out. Watch how her ability to track the ball improves each week. Make sure to play this game when your baby is in a state of quiet alertness

This type of monitor is often used on premature babies, allowing their parents to keep track of how their baby's immature lungs are functioning. These monitors may also be used with babies who have had episodes of apnea (periods where they stop breathing) or babies who have a family history of SIDS.

There are benefits and drawbacks to these more complex monitors. We used a sleep apnea monitor with our second baby. The alarm went off twice, and I felt like I lost ten years off my life each time! Of course, if your baby is at risk for any breathing-related distress and your pediatrician has recommended a respiratory monitor, the potential benefits far outweigh any potential drawbacks, such as dealing with wires, machinery, and false alarms.

Video and sound monitors might give anxious parents peace of mind, but they can have drawbacks, too. Stories abound of private conversations or moments that were overheard or unintentionally viewed by unsuspecting bystanders when parents forgot there was a monitor on in the nursery!

and stop when she turns her head away or no longer follows the ball with her eyes.

GET UP AND GO: GROSS MOTOR SKILLS

From the moment your baby is born, he begins working on his gross motor skills. It's important that you support your baby's head and neck during the first few weeks as he gains control of the muscles in his neck. As your baby grows, he

Dottie Says

"It's never too early to start pampering yourself. A gentle massage feels wonderful and really relaxes me. I love to hear my mommy's voice and feel her gentle touch. I can really tell how much she loves me."

The language of touch is the first language that your baby will understand. Massage can calm and soothe your baby as it communicates your love and care for her. Your hospital or birth center may offer postpartum baby massage classes, which are a wonderful way to meet other new mothers while gaining confidence in your newborn massage technique.

Your baby should be naked to enjoy a massage. Since many new babies don't like the feeling of being naked, use a light blanket to cover the parts of her body you are not touching. If you like, you may use a light massage oil on your baby's body, or you may use just your hands. Make sure you warm your hands before touching your baby. Talk or sing to

develops muscle control from the top down. He begins by learning to balance his head, which is quite heavy relative to the rest of his body weight, and then to control his arm movements, and then to control his legs. Really, it's just a matter of strength, coordination, and practice before the floppy-headed infant in your arms develops into the creeping, crawling, walking, and running tornado that will whirl through your house over the next several years.

As your baby begins to gain greater control over his body, you can help him figure out how it all comes to-her during the massage, telling her what you are doing. In the first month, be sure to use a very gentle touch. When your baby is older, you can exert more pressure. Once you have touched your baby, keep at least one hand in contact with her until the massage is over. Don't massage your baby's tummy if she's just eaten, and be sensitive to her reactions. If she does not seem to be enjoying the massage, stop right away. You can always try again when she is a few weeks older.

If she is enjoying the massage, you can vary the strokes you use. Try rubbing in light circles or stroking from top to bottom. Here are some other motions you can try:

- stroking with an open palm
- stroking with just your fingers
- lightly "raking" with your fingertips
- gently tapping with your fingertips
- massaging arms and legs with a gentle "wringing" motion

gether by doing such simple things as changing his position. He can't move himself from side to side, or from back to stomach, but he may enjoy the different perspective and feeling of these different positions. Always make sure you support your baby on his side by placing a rolled-up receiving blanket or cloth diaper on either side of him, so he does not unexpectedly roll backward or onto his face. Never leave your baby unattended during "tummy time" or allow him to lie facedown on any soft surface or blanket.

Another way you can help your baby become comfortable in her skin is through movement. Experiment with walking, dancing, rocking, or gentle bouncing while holding your baby to allow her to experience the sensation of moving through space. Be careful to support her head and keep her body close to yours so she feels secure. If she seems agitated, try slower or smoother movements. Short, abrupt movements may startle or confuse some babies.

GAMES

Shall We Dance?

Put on a CD and waltz around the room with your tiny dance partner. Change the music and try a rocking cha-cha step. Experiment to see what pleases your baby, whether it's a rhythmic bounce to some rock and roll, or a gentle glide to a composition by Debussy. The Baby Prodigy *Musical Pacifier* CD series is a perfect accompaniment for a pas de deux. One baby I know was comforted without fail by a free-spirited sixties-style whirl around the living room to John Lennon's "Free as a Bird." Make sure that the music is not too loud and that your baby feels securely supported as you dance.

chapter three

Meet the Real Me:
Two through Three Months

My husband and I were wondering when our baby was going to do something exciting. After putting up with weeks and weeks of sleepless nights, I felt like a cute baby trick would be the least he could do for me. One day, when he was about ten weeks old, I was taking him out for a stroll and I stopped to admire a dog. I said, "Look, honey, it's a doggie!" He looked right at me and gave me the biggest smile. He did something for me, all right—he completely melted my heart.

Beverly, Connor's mom

WELCOME TO YOUR NEW LIFE

As you slowly emerge from the sleepless daze of the past four weeks and begin to get into the groove of this whole parenting thing, you'll be delighted to discover that the adorable tiny bundle you brought home from the hospital is becoming a curious and interactive little person. These early months give you a taste of what is to come as your baby begins to express her desire to learn more about the world.

As your baby begins to study her environment in earnest, you may begin to feel pressured to be the best teacher you can be. You may suddenly start noticing all the products offered in various baby catalogs and become overwhelmed by the wide range of "educational" toys on the market today. But don't get too stressed out about how to ensure your budding genius graduates with honors from the college of her choice. In fact, you are probably doing— quite naturally—many of the things that most effectively promote brain development. What's important to remember, especially with infants at this stage, is to avoid over-orchestration and overstimulation. At this age, and for the rest of your baby's early development, learning occurs just as much in informal activities as in structured ones.

SETTLING IN

As your baby matures, she will be able to maintain for longer periods of time the quiet alert stage I discussed in the last chapter. The number of interactive opportunities for stimulating your baby's senses and interests increases as her capacity for focus increases. Most of the activities suggested in the last chapter become more and more interesting for both you and your baby to play. As you stimulated your infant over the past four weeks, you were laying the groundwork in her memory for some of the games in this chapter.

Last month you may have felt like you were simply playing with and talking to a very beautiful little doll. Over the next few months, try some of the same games and see what an interactive little partner you now have. A baby who tracks a black-and-white plush toy when he is three weeks old may be eagerly reaching for the same toy when he is nine weeks old. The slippery little fish who at three weeks would wriggle and fuss in the bath now begins to calm down as soon as you begin to sing his special bath-time song.

The shared enjoyment you and your baby are experiencing is laying the groundwork for your child's social development. Toward the end of three months, stuffed toys become a great tool for strengthening baby's early social skills. When you chat with teddy bears or converse with stuffed elephants, you are modeling communication skills and setting the stage for those long babbling conversations between older babies and their precious plush friends.

Your baby's growing interest in objects and people will begin to expand to the world beyond his nursery. Start getting baby out and exposing him to the whole big world. Your baby will still love being in a carrier or sling, which gives him a feeling of security, while he is exploring a whole new sensory experience. One mother who raised her young daughter in New York City took the opportunity of running errands to introduce her daughter to the world.

She did all of her chores by bus or subway, so her daughter could enjoy a vast array of sights, sounds, and smells. When the baby had had enough, she would simply turn her face into her mother's chest and have a nap.

You don't have to live in a city to give your baby a wide range of experiences. If you live in a suburban area where you need to drive, then drive to a park or to the mall, put the baby in a front carrier, and take a stroll as he absorbs all the different sensations. If the weather permits, take your baby outside in the stroller. If the weather's lousy, choose an indoor location, such as the mall, or take a tour of your house. Even just standing and looking out the window with him will give your baby something new to focus on.

Vary the type and amount of stimulation your baby is getting. As a rough rule of thumb, you'll want to provide your baby with opportunities for stimulation during *at least half* of his waking hours. Make sure that the activities range from low key and soothing to more stimulating and exciting.

Different areas of your baby's skills develop more noticeably at different ages. From one to three months, the gross motor skill development is very easily apparent. Head control improves, as does posture—your baby no longer scrunches up into a little ball at every opportunity. Kicking is an exciting new exercise. Your baby's hands are a constant source of wonder and interest, too, as your child now learns she can move them in and out of the range of her vision and, shortly thereafter, that she can reach for the things that interest her.

Dottie Says

"I love it when Mommy takes me with her on her morning runs. Sitting in the jogging stroller is a great way to watch the whole big world go by."

Jogging with your baby is great exercise for you and an exciting outing for her. But make sure you always use the right equipment, and be sure her head and neck are well supported. At this age, your baby could suffer serious injuries if bounced or jostled vigorously. Avoid any bouncing activities that could shake or jar your baby's unsupported head or neck. Don't run with your baby in a front carrier or pack, and make sure to reject any roughhousing or physical games—like tossing baby up into the air—in favor of nonjarring activities.

SLEEPING AND WAKING

No promises, but toward the end of the third month, your baby may start sleeping through the night. Now, don't get too excited yet. I define "sleeping through the night" for a baby at this age as staying asleep for at least six consecutive hours. That means you may have a baby who wakes for a midnight feeding and then sleeps right through until just before six—or you may have a baby who wants to take his six hours between nine p.m. and three a.m. and then have company until he is ready for an early morning nap around six a.m. Unfortunately, "sleeping through the night" almost never means you can log the eight blissful hours of solid sleep you enjoyed pre-baby!

Did You Know?: Hiring a Caregiver

Now that your baby is nearing three months old, I want to briefly talk about caregivers other than you or your partner. Whether you will be returning to work or are simply hoping to have an occasional babysitter, you will need to make the important decision of who will care for your baby when you are not able to be with him. I talk about this more in the next chapter, but to get you started thinking about what your baby needs from caregivers other than his parents, consider the following:

- All caregivers are an important part of your child's development and learning.

- Warm and caring relationships with adults provide children with the basis for all types of learning.

- Caregivers should see everyday caring routines as opportunities for expanding a child's brainpower.

- You should allow yourself about six to eight weeks to hire someone.

- Plan to spend time with a new caregiver before having her fly solo, so you can observe how she interacts with your baby and get used to the way she does things. (Which might not be the same way *you* would do it, but you do have to be comfortable with her style.)

- Communicate an attitude of trust in the caregiver. Your baby will take his cues from you.

If you will be placing your child in home or institutional day care, or plan on hiring a caregiver before the end of the third month, skip ahead to the next chapter to read about what to look for in all kinds of child-care situations.

At this age, a baby who is following a textbook course of development (and congratulations if yours is—I hope you know how lucky you are!) would wake about the same time each morning, eat, stay awake for a bit, nap, wake again, enjoy lunch, then have another nap followed by a longer period of afternoon wakefulness, eat "dinner" and take an evening nap before waking for the last feed of the night, and then go back to bed for six (or more) hours of sleep.

Even if your baby hasn't read that particular book, the good news is that as his patterns of eating, sleeping, and waking become more apparent, you can encourage a more regular schedule by actively managing the different parts of your baby's day: wakings, feedings, naps, outings, and baths. Try to ensure that these activities occur at or near the same times every day. Start stretching the periods between feedings by getting the baby interested in other things. After a feeding, instead of letting your baby drop off to sleep, try to engage him in an activity you know he enjoys.

Most parenting books have extensive sections on sleep that apply to babies at this age. There are many different approaches, and you can do some research and come up with the method that works best for your family and your baby.

STIMULATING YOUR BABY

As I've already mentioned, most parents naturally do the things that provide infants with stimulating environments

The Midnight Diaper: To Change or Not to Change

It's possible that by now you have been able to master the unobtrusive diaper change: super speedy and done in dim light. If you have this skill, then your baby may not even twitch once she falls asleep after a feeding. You can always change her diaper before you begin the middle-of-the-night feeding, although you then risk a crying jag that can disturb the whole household.

And so I'd like to propose a radical diapering strategy that lets everyone get back into bed in pursuit of those six straight hours of blissful shut-eye: Dare to skip that midnight diaper change! As long as there is no poop, simply scoop your baby out of bed, feed her, and slide her back into her crib. Disposable diapers are superduper absorbent, and will keep moisture away from baby's skin until she awakens you for her early morning feeding. Of course, if your baby has a dirty diaper, or a diaper rash or other skin condition, you'll have to continue with late-night diaper changes along with the late-night feedings. But in order to promote a trend toward sleeping through the night, don't stimulate your baby during these feedings by chatting, turning on lights or music, or playing games. Sit quietly, let baby eat in as sleepy a fashion as possible, and slip her back into bed.

for growth. You're probably not even aware of the daily things you do that all work together to help to stimulate your baby and reinforce the connections in her brain that are forming daily.

Just for fun, here's a short list of some of the things you

Taking a Bottle

If you are breast-feeding, now is a good time to get your baby started on accepting a bottle. It is undeniably useful to be able to leave an occasional feeding to someone else. If you are planning to go back to work, and even if you intend to pump breast milk, someone else will have to give your baby a bottle or two during the day. Some babies have no trouble switching between breast and bottle, but others are fussier about the switch.

Here are a few tips to make acceptance of the bottle easier for both of you:

- Start to offer a bottle (either breast milk or formula) somewhere around six to eight weeks.

- Wait until your baby is hungry, but not frantically so.

- Have a substitute feeder—someone other than baby's Mom—offer the bottle. (In fact, Mom, it's probably best if you leave the room, if not the house. Remember, your baby's acute sense of smell will let her know if her preferred milk source is nearby!)

- When offering the baby a bottle, cuddle her and maintain eye contact, just as when she nurses.

- Don't let one successful bottle-feeding make you complacent. Even if you are primarily breast-feeding, offer a bottle once or twice a week. As your baby gets older, he will become more willful—and possibly pickier. If he is not used to the bottle, he may reject it outright.

do that provide your baby with positive stimulation. See how much you do without even trying!

* **Love:** *Of course I love my baby* is what you are probably thinking, but treating your baby with loving care makes her feel secure. A secure baby is more willing to explore her environment and to initiate interactions. The tone of voice, the quality of touch, and the focused attention that a loving parent lavishes on his or her child is the cornerstone of your baby's happiness and confident development.

* **Relate:** Be sure to relate to your baby on a level she can understand. Simple explanations of daily activities stimulate the connections between actions and words. Your baby is a learning machine. Understanding your baby's cues and being responsive to her needs foster security and, later, independence.

* **Appreciate your baby's character:** Your baby is a unique individual—one that you as a parent no doubt find endlessly delightful and entertaining. How you respond to his own particular quirks and charms shapes his experience of the world. Always be appreciative of your baby's abilities, and have positive expectations for his development.

* **Have fun:** Every time you play with your baby, you create a new learning experience. So go ahead: indulge yourself and him with silly songs, games, or

funny voices or by dancing around a room or rolling on the floor.

* **Give space:** Quickly learn to read your baby's cues to understand when she has had enough stimulation. As you become attuned to your baby's thresholds for stimulation, you know when to politely tell Aunt Jane that her favorite niece has had enough "kootchy-coo" for one morning. You also give your baby "space" in another sense of the word by providing a secure environment for her ongoing explorations.

* **Let baby be boss:** You pick up your son when he cries; you soothe your daughter when she is fussy. Let your baby tell you what he needs, then follow your instincts.

* **Realize that timing is everything:** Whenever you respond promptly to your baby's request, you facilitate the connections in your baby's brain that govern cause and effect. You learn to judge your baby's states of alertness and drowsiness and can then play with her and soothe her at the right times.

* **Use positive reinforcement:** More good cause-and-effect training here! Your enthusiastic support of everything from burps to tummy rolls sets the tone for a lifetime of encouraging your child to explore his developing skills.

Simply by being an attentive and responsive parent you are doing exactly what your child needs to reinforce the neural connections and pathways that are rapidly forming

Games Siblings Play

It's almost impossible to predict how your older child may react to the realization that the newest member of the family is settled in for the long haul. Articulate toddlers may tell you that they'd like the baby to go back to the hospital. Older siblings may not exhibit any signs of jealousy and may, in fact, be overzealous in their attempts to care for "their" new baby. You can expect to walk the fine line of meeting all your children's needs for your time and attention for the rest of your life. But right now, there are a few things you can do to help everyone bond and adjust to their new relationships as brothers and sisters.

The most important thing you can do is stress to your older child that the love in your family isn't divided between each person in the family; rather it just keeps growing bigger to accommodate everyone.

in her developing brain. Raising a smarter, happier baby is easy once you understand that simply caring for your child in a warm and responsive way provides positive benefits in these important early years.

BABY STEPS

From the end of the first month to the end of the third month, your baby begins making the huge developmental leaps that you will continue to marvel at—probably for the rest of her life!

Remember that you have bonded with your baby through caregiving, so it's perfectly logical that allowing an older sibling to help with basic baby care will help to forge a stronger bond between them. Allow an older child to help with feeding, burping, diapering, and bathing as much as he is able. An older child can be a "babysitter," watching or playing with the baby as she sits in her bouncy chair or lies in her crib.

Let your older child "help" the baby by opening baby gifts and showing the baby any new toys. (It's perfectly fine for the older child to try out the toy for the baby!)

Teach your older child how to show things to the baby slowly, allowing the baby time to study them carefully. Let the older child show the baby his books, games, and schoolwork. Make sure he understands the baby's way of showing appreciation: with smiles and long intent gazes. Monitor the interactions carefully to help your older child learn the signals for when the baby has had enough stimulation.

By the end of two months, your child should achieve the milestones listed below. If you are concerned about your child's rate of development, consult your pediatrician.

During the second month, your baby should be able to:

* smile back at you when you smile
* respond to a noise with a startle, by crying, or by becoming quiet
* vocalize by cooing (rather than crying)
* track an object held directly above her face
* lift her head while on her stomach

* hold her head steady
* pay attention to a very small object
* grab hold of an object held to the tips of her fingers
* reach for an object

It is possible that by the end of the second month, your baby may:

* lift her head 90 degrees while on her stomach
* laugh

Dookie Says

"Why won't this big person leave me alone? He keeps leaning in close to me and talking loudly. I try looking away, but that just makes him pick me up and bounce me around. When I start to cry, he shows me toy after toy after toy. I can't even concentrate on them all. Oh, I don't want to play like this. I think I'm going to scream!"

An important thing for you to remember, as you try some of the suggestions in this chapter for stimulating your baby, is to pay close attention to your baby's signals. Make sure the stimulation you are offering is age-appropriate. It's easy to tell when you're on the right track: Your baby will be smiling and engaged. If he starts to look bored, bothered, or bewildered, gear down. Give him a couple of minutes to collect himself while you flip back a few chapters and find a simpler activity to try. Remember, stimulating or soothing your baby needs to be fun and satisfying for both of you.

Toy Chest

Now that your baby is spending more time awake and interested in her surroundings, you can expand your repertoire of entertainment devices. You will want to have a number of options for your baby to explore during the day. When choosing toys for your baby at this age, consider the following:

- Is this a toy that soothes or stimulates?
- What senses does this toy stimulate?
- Is this toy something he can watch or something he can actively play with?

Although your baby will now really appreciate a wider variety of toys, you don't have to clean out your local toy store. You can create toys that will fascinate your baby by using simple household items. When using household items, be sure they are safe. Your baby is approaching the age where her mouth is as important for exploring as her hands. From this point on, your baby will consider any object a plaything—an exciting new toy to be handled and explored. You'll need to ensure that there are no sharp edges, objects are not too tiny, and the things you don't want her to handle are out of range. Flip ahead to the next chapter for more specific tips on safe toys.

Here are some of my favorite ways to turn household items into toys:

- Spoons (shiny), keys (jingly), and tassels (brightly colored) can be clipped securely to an elastic and strung above your baby's head in her crib. Your baby will happily stare at this homemade mobile—and you can change objects as often as you like.

- Light and colorful things like aluminum pie plates, decorated paper plates, and ribbon streamers move easily in air currents. When your baby is able to swipe at objects, she will enjoy making these kinds of things swing and sway.

- A mirror gives your baby the opportunity to study an object she still finds fascinating: a face. (However, she won't recognize herself until around fifteen months.)

- Make a paper plate maraca (see p. 73.) and hold it where your baby can see it as she listens to the rhythmic shaking.

If you simply can't resist temptation as you pass a children's shop (and what parent can?), here are some suggestions for toys that your baby will enjoy both now and in the coming months:

- rattles or toys that make sounds
- toys that light up or flash or change color
- CDs of classical music or children's lullabies
- plush animals with different textures: shaggy, smooth, scaly

* follow an object from one side to the other
* smile without being prompted

By the end of the third month, your baby should be able to do all of the above and may also be able to:

* lift her chest off the ground by using her arms while on her tummy
* roll over (one way)

Safety Watch: Infant CPR

One of the most important things you can do to ensure your child's safety is to take an infant CPR class. Check with your hospital to see if it offers one for new parents. The CPR technique for babies under one year differs from the one for babies one year and older, so plan to take a refresher course when your baby turns one.

* turn toward your voice
* blow a raspberry
* keep head level as she is pulled into a sitting position

BABY TALK

By the end of the third month your baby is realizing that he lives in a world made up of sounds. He's also beginning to make the connection that all these sounds mean something. By now you have probably become adept at interpreting your child's cries. You can easily tell when he is hungry, uncomfortable, or tired, and you can respond promptly and correctly. As he becomes confident that his needs are being met, he will begin experimenting with other types of communication.

The way you communicate with your baby is shifting. You now need to talk *with* instead of *at* your child. Quite

Your Baby's View: When Enough Is Enough!

Imagine this scenario: You're at a party and find yourself trapped behind the buffet table with the most dreaded of all party guests: the close-talking boor.

She leans in and rapid-fires question after question at you—"How *are* you? Where's your precious baby? Have you gotten him to sleep through the night yet? No? Do you want to know what I did? Where did you get those adorable shoes?" Your head begins to ache. You answer in a monotone, with curt sentences.

She presses closer. "Here, try some of this ham salad. Oh, you're a vegetarian? Well, have some bean dip. No? What's the matter—you're not hungry? Try some finger sandwiches. Go on—try one bite." You glance away and maybe take a step backward.

She's relentless. She moves closer still and grabs your arm. "Here, look at pictures of our family vacation. See, there's Ralph doing the hula. And here's little Suzy's ballet rehearsal." This time you turn your whole body away and wave at a friend across the room. You don't want to be rude, but if she doesn't give you some space, you're going to have to say something—or even simply walk away.

Now imagine that you're trapped at this same party, with the same ill-mannered guest. But you can't talk, or wave to your friend to rescue you, or walk away. The next time your baby gives you a signal that your attentions have become overpowering, be a polite parent and excuse yourself from the party, before you force your baby to be rude.

simply, babies who are talked to a great deal become talkative. You can still continue a running commentary as you move through your day, as I suggested in the previous chapter, but now you need to pause occasionally, listen to the input from your tiny audience, and respond to his "comments." At this age, babies are very interested in repetition, tone, and cadence. And by using your body—gestures and facial expressions—you make whatever you are saying even more compelling.

The interactions you have with your baby at this age lay the foundation for her social talking. Your baby will soon get the idea that conversation is a two-way street. And the more social talking a baby experiences, the more practice talking she will attempt on her own time. Over the next few months, her sound making may take on a conversational rhythm with pauses and repeated tones and sounds.

When chatting with your baby, don't oversimplify what you are saying. Speak conversationally and be sure to pause to allow for a reply. If you really want a big response, use a higher-pitched voice or a singsong tone (called "parentese" in some parenting books). Babies are more responsive to a voice with this sound, and soon you should be rewarded with a wide range of coos, gurgles, and giggles, often accompanied by gestures and wriggles as your baby jumps into the conversation with you.

Of course, reading to your baby is another way to stimulate the language centers of her brain. By three months, a baby can pay attention to pictures in books and will enjoy sitting on your lap as you name the objects on the page. In the bookshelf section of this chapter, I suggest several books with simple, colorful illustrations and rhythmic language that should capture your child's attention.

Most important of all, *listen* to your baby and respond verbally each time he makes noises at you. And remember, when your baby becomes quiet, closes his eyes or looks away, or begins to fuss, he's telling you he's had enough chatter for the moment. Be respectful and spend some time in a companionable silence.

GAMES

The Name Game

Pointing and naming games are of great interest to babies of this age. It's an especially good game to play with body parts. By doing this, you can incorporate two other important learning tools: questions and gestures. When your baby is in a quiet alert stage, begin by pointing to a part of your face—the part of your body your baby is most interested in looking at at this age. Ask her "What's this?" as you point at your nose. Expect a look of intense concentration as she takes in your question. "This is Mommy's nose," you tell her. And then touch her on the nose. "And this is baby's nose." Watch as she begins to anticipate both the question and the touch.

And Today's Guest Is . . .

Make like a talk show host and interview your baby. Use a high-pitched voice to ask your questions, and then wait for him to reply before translating his answer for the studio audience. Add gestures: pretend you're holding a microphone up to him as you wait for a reply. If his "answer" is astonishing or hilarious, exaggerate your response.

A Classic Crowd-Pleaser

Incorporate touch and language by playing games like "This Little Piggy." Or sing "Itsy-Bitsy Spider," using your fingers to walk up your baby's tummy as the spider crawls up the waterspout and trailing your fingertips down his body to illustrate "down came the rain." Be creative and discover how many other nursery rhymes and songs lend themselves to a multisensory experience.

The Echo Game

Wait for your baby to make a specific sound—not a cry or a grunt, but a coo or a gurgle. Imitate the noise back to him. It's likely he will mimic the noise back to you again. Vary the tone of your voice as you imitate each noise he makes. Soon you'll begin to feel as if you're carrying on a conversation—in a second language you didn't even know you spoke: baby-ese.

THE LITTLE THINGS: FINE MOTOR SKILLS

As your baby's motor control has developed, she has discovered to her delight that there are fascinating little things attached to the ends of her arms. These entertaining objects weave in and out of her field of vision and sometimes even find their way into her mouth. Yes—your baby has discovered her hands. At first her hand movements are totally random, but as the weeks go by, she will

Bookshelf

When you sneak out for that rare escape to a nearby bookstore or, better yet, bookstore/café, you will find a slew of books that will be appropriate for your one- to three-month-old. Here I offer general guidelines and a few of my specific favorites. Be prepared to read some of these over and over again, as they might become well-loved favorites that your baby may demand for months and months before moving on.

Keep in mind that by two months, babies can focus on and pay attention to pictures in a book. They don't know what the pictures actually mean, but this is a first step in emergent literacy.

Books for You
- *Baby Mind: Brain-Building Games Your Baby Will Love* by Linda Acredolo, Ph.D., and Susan Goodwyn, Ph.D.

Books to Enjoy with Your Baby
- Board books with photos of other babies that can be propped up on crib or blanket
- Small plastic photo albums of family and friends
- *Color Zoo* by Lois Ehlert
- *Baby Shapes* by Helen Dorman
- *Freight Train* by Donald Crews
- *Big Red Barn* by Margaret Wise Brown
- *Tickle, Tickle* by Helen Oxenbury
- *Pretty Brown Face* by Andrea and Brian Pinkney

Books for Your Older Child
- *Julius, the Baby of the World* by Kevin Henkes

be able to move her hands more purposefully. Even if your baby enjoyed being swaddled as a newborn, it's important now that you leave her hands free so that her random hand movements can become controlled. From eight to ten or twelve weeks of age, toys that are light, easy to grasp, and make some sound can help your baby establish a connection between herself and her hands.

As your baby begins to explore his ability to control his hands in order to touch something he is looking at, you can help him make the connection by purchasing or making lightweight fabric rattles that can fasten around his wrists. As he waves his arms around, the noise will capture his attention and direct his eyes to what his hands are doing.

After twelve weeks, your baby no longer needs the noise to direct his attention to his hands; he knows exactly where they are and is intent on watching them. As he practices bringing his hands together in front of his face, then spreading them apart, then moving them out of sight, you can offer him opportunities to enhance his fine motor skills by handing him objects and letting him explore different sounds and textures.

Your baby will use his hands to explore things through tactile sensation. You'll notice that although he becomes more and more accurate at reaching out to touch objects, he still has trouble picking them up. It will be several months before he develops the ability to use his fingers and thumb in the pincer grip that lets him manipulate smaller objects. At about three months he will use a two-handed approach to trapping objects, dragging them toward himself, often between his wrists, then scooping them up with his palms.

Offer him a variety of surfaces to explore: rugs, fabrics, smooth and rough surfaces. Attach an activity board to the side of his crib. He may only swipe at it for now, but it offers all kinds of tactile, visual, and tonal stimulation.

GAMES

Mini Conductor

Allow your baby to grasp your forefingers in her fists. Slowly move your hands back and forth, up and down. She will follow the movement of her hands with great interest. Add some music (of course we like the Baby Prodigy *Musical Pacifier* CD series!), and ta-da—your baby's conducting her first symphony.

Silk and Satin, Leather and Lace

Scraps of fabric give your baby a chance to explore different sensations. Offer him a washcloth or a blanket with a smooth satin edge. Let him lie on the leather couch in the living room (and stay right next to him, because if you glance away for even a minute, I guarantee that will be the moment your little darling learns to roll over!) or hand him a plush animal. At first he may grasp the objects in his fist, but in a few months he will be able to feel the different fabrics more sensitively, using his fingertips.

HOW IT ALL FITS: SPATIAL DEVELOPMENT

Like a camera coming into focus, your baby's vision improves at two months, then again at four months, and finally reaches 20/20 at or around six months. Before three months, infants see best with their peripheral vision. They notice movement and can appreciate high-contrast patterns. Many of the games from the previous chapter will continue to delight your two-month-old. As her vision continues to develop, your baby becomes increasingly aware of her environment and able to study things by staring right at them. She can now follow objects that move in a circle (like mobiles). Our oldest daughter was absolutely fascinated by the ceiling fan. We would turn it on at high speed, at low speed, with the light fixture on or off. I even added a brightly colored tassel to the pull string. It was good for at least five minutes of silence as she stared wide-eyed at the rotating fan, as if hypnotized. Later, she would wave her arms toward the ceiling, like she was carrying on a sign-language dialogue with the whirring blades.

Now that your baby is aware of the visual world around her, you need to ensure that she has something interesting to look at. I'm not recommending that you rush out and buy mobiles or mirrors or picture books and cover every inch of your baby's waking environment. Remember, *all* objects are new to your baby, so she will enjoy almost anything you show or hand to her. Color, shape, sound, and weight are what make things interesting to babies. Remember, too, that you do not want to overstimulate your child. Don't offer more than one or two objects at a time, and be alert for any signs that your little one has had enough stimulation.

Here's a short list of common household sights and objects to get you thinking about what kind of everyday things can provide visual stimulation for your child.

* shadows on painted walls
* venetian blinds
* ceiling fans
* faces
* white paper plates with simple black or red shapes or simple faces

Your baby is still attracted to black-and-white images, but as he approaches the end of his third month, he is growing more attracted to some primary colors, especially red. A study headed by Dr. Melanie J. Spence at the University of Texas at Dallas School of Human Development showed that infants of three months are able to differentiate between black and white and primary colors and that they prefer red and yellow over blue and green.

Along with an improvement in their vision, babies also begin to experience an improvement in their ability to control the movements of their arms and hands. As I discussed above, your baby will find her hands endlessly interesting. This interest in looking at things and reaching for things is the beginning of hand-eye coordination.

By the end of the third month, your baby will be able to purposely swipe at things. Toys such as a woolly ball can be strung up above his crib, so the ball is about ten inches from his face. He probably will not yet reach for these toys with the intent of grabbing them. Right now he's still concentrating on making those unpredictable hands and arms move the way he wants them to! He will bat at the ball, sometimes connecting with it to make it swing. You can also hang a light rattle as well. The sound, combined with the movement when he makes contact, will be very satisfying to him indeed.

In addition to mastering hand-eye coordination, your baby is on the way to developing his understanding of cause and effect!

GAMES

Playing Catch

Hold a brightly colored ball about twelve inches away from your baby's face and just below eye level. (A ball that squeaks or has a bell is even better for capturing his attention.) Watch as your baby looks first at his hands and then at the ball, and then brings his hands together to clasp the ball. This exercise stimulates hand-eye coordination. Entertain your baby and yourself by adding your best sports announcer's play-by-play: "Sam goes deep in center field. He sizes up the hit; he's looking at his glove, the ball, his glove . . . and . . . what a grab! He's got it, ladies and gentlemen! That's the third out and Team Baby wins the World Series."

Shake Your Booties

Treat your baby to a low-tech rhythm section by making maracas. Set two paper plates face-to-face, then staple around the edges of the plates, fastening them together but leaving an opening at the top. Fill with dried rice, beans, or seeds. Staple the opening securely shut and decorate the plates with bold colors and simple shapes. Keep the beat to your own singing, or shake along with a favorite CD selection. Don't let your baby get her hands on this instrument, however; she could open it, and the filling could be a choking hazard.

GET UP AND GO: GROSS MOTOR SKILLS

As your baby's control over her body moves downward, from head to feet, she begins to develop more strength in her torso. She enjoys being propped up in a sitting position, but you need to be careful. Until she is five or six months old, she will probably gradually slump or slide down in the place where you have propped her, and will be unable to wriggle back up into a comfortable position. Fabric "bouncing chairs" can provide her with exactly the kind of firm slope that allows her to sit up and see what's going on without collapsing over in a saggy heap! When she can lift her head and shoulders out of the chair, you can let her try supported sitting without the chair.

If you're using a bouncy chair you'll soon notice that your baby is also hard at work on mastering control of his legs. He'll quickly figure out that his legs, which used to jerk and twitch spastically, can now kick in a smooth and coordinated bicycle style.

As your child begins to develop his own personal physical-fitness program of kicking, arm waving, and rolling over, you need to be sure to provide him with plenty of opportunities to practice unrestricted movements. But be careful: Many parents have discovered their baby has mastered the new skill of rolling over only after they hear the distinctive thump and wail of a small body dropping off a bed as they stand nearby folding laundry! Allow for plenty of floor time (the safest place for practicing his rolling-over skills) and don't keep him cooped up in a stroller or baby seat. "Tummy time" is still important, as your baby works at strengthening his neck, shoulder, and forearm muscles.

GAMES

Ready for Takeoff

Let your baby fly! Hold her securely with her belly resting on the inside of your forearm and your hand cupping her chest. Drape one of her legs on either side of your arm and use your free hand for additional support. Slowly and smoothly at first, and then at varying speeds, move her away from and then back toward your body. Add interesting noises like whooshes and engine sounds as she waves her arms and legs and "flies" from place to place.

Seesaw

With your baby lying on his back, gently grasp his wrist and pull him upright to a sitting position. Make sure he is strong enough and has enough muscle control that he can hold his neck steady as you bring him up. Steady him in a sitting position for a few minutes, then slowly lower him back down. Add funny expressions to your face as you pull him toward you and sound effects as you lower him.

Safety Watch: Bathing Your Baby

While you may have been able to get through the first month of your baby's life with simple towel baths, the day has come when both you and your baby are confident enough to graduate to bathing in a baby tub or sink.

By about two months, most infants enjoy being naked and will kick and splash gleefully. Instead of tensing themselves against the water, babies now delight in the sensation of floating and are thrilled to learn that with the water supporting some of their weight, they can do their best and hardest kicking. This kind of gross motor stimulation is important for your baby's physical development and has the added benefit of leaving your baby relaxed and thoroughly exercised. Scheduling a bath before your baby's evening feeding can be beneficial in promoting a good night's sleep.

Although many parents may find bathing a squirming, slippery baby an intimidating prospect (I know I did!), a few simple tips can make bath time your baby's (and your) favorite time:

- A baby bathtub that can rest on the counter or fit in the sink will spare you backache. Or if you have a big enough sink in your kitchen or bathroom, you can pad the sink with towels to make a safe bathing place. Make sure that you turn the faucet away from your baby or wrap it with a washcloth to avoid scalding drips.

- Before beginning the bath, collect everything you need: towels, clean clothing, warm water.

- If you're still shaky about washing your baby's hair, undress him and swaddle him in a towel on your lap. Holding him on your lap or in a football hold (your hand supporting his head and neck, his body tucked under your arm), rinse his hair and wash his face.

- Support his head and neck with one hand, his bottom and thighs with the other, and lower him into the bath. Hold him while he gets used to it, then remove your hand from his bottom. Keep supporting his head and use your free hand to wash and play.

- Lift your baby from the tub by sliding your hand back under his bottom and gripping one of his thighs. Keep a good grip—he'll be slippery. Gently lay him down on a large, soft towel and pat him dry.

- Baby lotions are not necessary but can smell nice. You should never use talcum powder on your baby; if you want to use a powder, look for one with a cornstarch base.

Take Your Mark, Get Set . . .

Let your baby lie on her tummy on the floor. Place your hands behind her feet and let her push off against your palms. At first she'll probably just be flexing and strengthening her legs, but before you know it, she'll have coordinated her efforts and be able to push off and scoot forward on her chest. Toward the end of the third month, this is a great exercise to stimulate creeping, the precursor to crawling.

chapter four

An Eager Participant:
Four through Six Months

I was so happy the day that Debbie could sit on my lap and hold her head still to look at me. No more wobbling! Even more exciting was the day she could sit up and play. It doesn't seem that long ago that I would prop her up, and then have to run right over to stop her from tipping to one side. She seems so excited to explore her newfound abilities. I love watching her little hand reach out for her toys. And, at last, her big sister is able to play new kinds of games with her—games that are interesting to both of them! Debbie has so much more to do now that she sits up—and so do we.

Denise, Debbie and Daisy's mom

TIME FLIES

It's amazing to think that your baby is a quarter of the way to her first birthday already. All the adorable outfits you bought when she was first born no longer fit. She's wriggling out of the little plastic bathtub she used to be able to swim in. And after a full day of carrying her in the baby carrier, you need a few more yoga stretches to work the kinks out of your back before bedtime. It seems like every time you turn around, she's grown another inch or gained a few more pounds. But she's doing so much more than just adding upward spikes to the growth chart in her baby book. Even as you measure her physical progress, take the time to marvel at the amazing bounds she's made in emotional and intellectual development. The stimulation you provide in all your interactions with your child keep her entertained and engaged, even as important neuronal connections continue to be formed and enhanced.

Your baby's interest in the world at large is exploding. She's exploring her environment at a phenomenal pace—there's so much to discover and learn!

AN INTREPID EXPLORER

Over these next few months, you'll be able to add all kinds of milestones to the baby book as your child embarks on new adventures in eating, conversing, and playing. First foods, first "words," and first teeth are all introduced into your relationship. You'll also notice that your baby is more actively *initiating* interactions that stimulate all of his senses. He may be reaching out toward you, eagerly touching you, and exploring your mouth, nose, and ears with his finger. One father jokes that he was sure his son would grow up to be a dentist, given the baby's early and intense interest in exploring his father's molars for minutes at a time.

Your baby's vision and memory are becoming more strongly linked. He will begin looking for dropped objects—and expecting you to notice he has dropped something as well. He may begin showing caution or fear by turning away, crying, or clinging at the sound of strange voices or when exposed to new situations. His verbal communications become clearer as he makes his moods known by fussing, or by calming himself, more deliberately. And of course, his mouth becomes another tool in his ongoing quest for knowledge as he explores the taste and texture of everything he comes in contact with.

The activities and stimulation you provide as you interact with your baby during these months will serve as early lessons in cause and effect. At first it will dawn on your baby that she can elicit your smiles and attention by smiling or verbalizing. Later, as you offer her a rattle to hold, she'll figure out that shaking the toy causes it to make a sound. Still later, she'll realize that holding her arms out toward you results in being scooped up for a cuddle. What all this means for you is that you now have an active participant in the games that you've been playing all along. You'll notice that some of the activities suggested in this chapter are similar to those in the previous chapter. Repetition is an important part of solidifying the connections your baby is making through the activities you do with her each day. For newborns, the games I suggested in the previous chapters laid the foundation for the creation of early

Games Siblings Play

Much to your older child's interest and—I hope—delight, his baby sibling is turning into an interactive, admiring playmate. Your baby's smiles and laughs can charm her siblings as much as they charm you. Steer your older child toward rhyming or singing games where he can handle the actions and words and the baby can provide the appreciative audience. Some of the early favorites for toddler-led games in our household included:

- **Peekaboo.** The best of all the games in terms of eliciting a satisfying reaction from the baby.

- **Ring around the Rosie.** I would modify this game so that I held the baby in one arm and used my free hand to hold my older daughter's hand as we slowly spun in a circle. This works best when baby is in a front carrier. The "all fall down" part adds a greater thrill when you participate as well!

- **Old MacDonald.** You can provide the lyrics and leave the animal noises to the older child. It won't be long before the baby clamors to join in.

memories. Now you can build on those memories as you stimulate your older infant at a different level. Your relationship becomes more interactive each day, and it is important that you allow for your baby's participation. She will be eager to assert herself.

SLEEPING AND WAKING

I know you're hoping that this is the point where I tell you that your baby will be sleeping straight through the night. And I hate to disappoint you, but with two children of my own, I know better than to make any promises. What I *can* tell you is that by now, your baby may be sleeping up to eight consecutive hours each evening—and of course, we've all heard of those lucky parents whose little angels are consistently logging a solid twelve-hour stretch of shut-eye each night.

What is important at this stage of development is that you and your partner have a clear philosophy about sleep. You may decide that it's important to teach your baby how to fall asleep on her own and how to resettle herself if she wakes in the night. You may decide that you want to lull your child to sleep each night, singing lullabies and rubbing her back until she is soundly sleeping. You may decide that co-sleeping, which is also sometimes called a family bed, is the right approach for your family. There are many parenting books specifically devoted to the subject of children and sleep. I've listed a few in the appendix. Consult them for help in determining which method is best for you.

According to most baby books, the "average" baby, between the ages of three and six months, will sleep between fourteen and sixteen hours a day. Now repeat after me: "There is no such thing as an average baby!" Some babies need more sleep, some less. Your baby will establish her own routine, but I can offer you a few basic tips for enhancing good sleep habits:

* **Encourage longer, more regular naps with longer periods of wakefulness between them.** By the fifth month, your baby should be able to stay awake for about three and a half hours at a stretch. Help her expand her awake time by engaging her in activities she enjoys before offering her a feeding. Be careful not to overstimulate her when you *do* want her to go to sleep.

* **Keep to a schedule.** As much as possible, keep meals, outings, and baths at or around the same time each day. Routines will help your baby learn to anticipate what is expected of her.

* **Whenever possible, put your baby to sleep in his crib.** He will soon associate his crib with sleep.

* **Whenever possible, put your baby in his crib when he is drowsy, but still awake.** This will help him to learn to fall asleep on his own.

STIMULATING YOUR BABY

In every interaction with your child, you should be aware of how you can actively stimulate more than one of her senses and enhance all the connections that are forming. It may sound intimidating, but I want to reassure you that your natural instincts in caring for and playing with your child remain your best tools in enhancing and encouraging your baby's development.

At this important stage, when your baby is learning that he can have an effect on your behavior, it is important that you watch carefully and observe how your baby signals you. You may have a very outgoing baby who has great motor control and can use his body, such as by waving his hands or pointing, to express his desires. Or your baby may be a strong communicator who has developed a particular pattern of sounds to indicate what he wants. What's key here is observing the patterns of your baby's behavior and consistently and appropriately acknowledging what he is telling you through his nonverbal communications. Pay attention and learn what those grunts and hand waves mean to your baby, so you can react appropriately. Your reaction will reinforce the concept of cause and effect as well as increasing his ability to communicate—both important milestones.

Pay attention to what your baby likes to look at. She will be showing clear preferences at this age. Make sure she has interesting objects to focus her attention on in her immediate environment, but don't overwhelm her. She is still only able to really concentrate on one thing at a time.

From about six months on, your baby may be interested in observing moving objects, as long as the movement isn't too quick or jerky. Many parents introduce their children to DVDs or videos, like those in the Baby Prodigy series, at this time. The videos can focus their attention with classical music and show simple objects that they find interesting.

Your Baby's View

What if you were set loose in the most fascinating store in the world, stocked with merchandise that you just couldn't wait to explore? You might be staring at a table full of unbelievably cute shoes, or a counter full of beauty products, or a display of gourmet cookware, or a wall full of flat-screen TVs, or a gym full of high-tech exercise equipment . . . You get the idea. Of course you'd stare at all the items and maybe tentatively touch one or two. But you might feel overwhelmed by all there was to look at, to smell, to sample.

Finally, after agonizing deliberation, you decide. And from that moment you know what you want. You will not be deterred. You stride toward your prize, ready to claim it. You pick it up, admire it, and prepare to take it home.

And then someone comes over and snatches it from your hand. "No! No!" she exclaims loudly, talking to you as if you're simpleminded. "Don't touch that."

You're dumbfounded—and perhaps more than a little upset. *Well, what the heck did they show me all that stuff for?* you think as you head home, dejected and empty-handed.

This is how your baby may feel when set loose in your home. Before offering your baby a confounding array of choices, be sure that you are willing to hand over whatever he finally chooses as most interesting. Nobody likes to be tempted and then denied!

Sit with your baby while he watches a video or DVD and observe his reactions carefully. If he is smiling and engaged, he is ready for age-appropriate video entertainment. If he becomes fussy, turns away, or cries, he is overstimulated by the changing images, and you need to gear down and find his level of comfort with visual stimuli.

Over the next few months, your baby's responses will grow more selective. She will turn her head in the directions of sounds she prefers. She will reserve her high-wattage grins for the people she loves best. Your baby's actions will also become more deliberate. This is a direct result of ongoing fine-tuning of the neuronal pathways that play a role in organized and purposeful communication. Although these changes may be the most remarkable that you observe in your baby during these few months, they are only a few of several areas undergoing important development.

BABY STEPS

From the beginning of the fourth month to the end of the sixth month, your baby will make significant progress, especially in the area of gross motor control. The skills he develops over these three months are the skills that he needs to crawl, walk, run, and climb, so enjoy the little bundle in your arms while you can.

By the end of the sixth month, your child should have achieved the milestones listed below. If you are concerned about your child's rate of development, consult your pediatrician.

Feeding Your Baby: Starting Solids

Depending on your pediatrician's recommendations, at some time between your baby's fourth and sixth months, you will get the go-ahead to begin introducing solid foods. In the first few months of solid feedings, the amount of food your baby consumes is secondary to the *experience* of learning about different eating techniques (spoon versus fingers), flavors and textures, and the social aspects of mealtimes.

Before you can introduce the first bite of baby cereal, your baby must be able to sit upright unsupported and be able to swallow rather than suck. Don't worry if your baby isn't too interested in eating at first, and never force a baby who isn't interested to continue to eat.

It's easy to find advice on what to feed your baby. There are baby cookbooks for those people who want to prepare all of their baby's first meals by hand. There are prepared baby foods that are organic or all-natural. Your friends with babies of their own might offer advice as, no doubt, will family members. Your pediatrician can also set you on the right

Between the beginning of the fourth month and the end of the fifth month, your baby should be able to:

* lift her head upright when lying on her stomach
* laugh
* follow an object as it is moved above her face from one side to the other
* hold her head steady

track. The next chapter will talk a bit about good early finger foods, but for now, here's a list of general tips that I found handy when first introducing solids to my children:

- **Gruel is great.** Yes, Oliver Twist may have grown weary of it, but a very thinned-out version of cereal is your best bet for pleasing early eaters. I used rice cereal thinned with breast milk until it wasn't much thicker than soup.

- **One for you, one for me.** Spoons, that is. Your baby will be as interested in grabbing the spoon as she is in the food that's on it. If you're really serious about getting the food into her, provide a second spoon for her entertainment between bites.

- **Bowls of cereal are easily confused with finger paints.** If you want to discourage your baby from splashing around in her dinner, keep the bowl close to you. She'll be just as happy drawing patterns on her tray with the drips that fall from the spoon!

- **The bigger the bib, the better.** Enough said. Except that you may also want to wear an apron to protect you from the inevitable swat that sends a spoonful of cereal flying.

* roll over
* grasp a rattle
* reach for an object
* make a razzing sound
* bear some weight on her legs when supported
* turn in the direction of a voice
* verbalize a few vowel-consonant combinations

By the end of the sixth month, your baby should be able to:

* sit without being supported
* stand if holding on to something
* pass an object from hand to hand
* pick up a small object in a pincer grasp
* babble steadily in vowel-consonant combinations
* feed herself a cracker or piece of cereal
* say "ma-ma-ma" and "da-da-da" (although not discriminately)

Dookie Says

"I don't understand why Daddy gets so frustrated at dinnertime. This stuff they're giving me is so interesting. When I try to grab it, it just squishes through my fingers. I can draw on my tray with it, too. And the spoon! It's so much fun to wave it around and it makes a great noise when I bang it on the table. Daddy just keeps saying "No!" and pushing my hands away and taking the spoon. I guess this eating thing is not as fun for him as it is for me!"

No parent wants to raise a child without manners. But the early days of feeding solids are not the time to be a stickler for Emily Post's rules of etiquette. Remember that your baby is now capable of integrating multiple senses to learn about new experiences. Eating and playing with food or utensils is a part of that process. Be sure to make your child's early exposure to mealtimes a positive experience. Believe me, you'll have years and years during which you can remind him to take his elbows off the table during dinner!

Heigh-Ho, Heigh-Ho! It's Off to Work We Go

For many working parents, the beginning of the fourth month signals a return to work and a need for high-quality child care for their baby. Deciding on another person to take care of your baby when you are not able to will be one of the most important decisions you make as a parent. One of the most common worries is that your baby will come to love her daily caregiver more than she loves you, her parents. I want to reassure you that no matter how much your baby loves her alternative caregiver, she will always love you in a completely unique way. The bond that you have created by interacting and stimulating your baby over the early months of her life is unbreakable.

However, your child's attachment to his caregivers is vital to his development. Studies show that babies attach to the people who give them companionship and stimulation, not necessarily to people who attend only to their physical needs. You have spent the last few months consciously stimulating your baby in natural ways that will enhance his potential and development. You *know* what your baby needs to be smarter and happier, and it is important that you find a child-care situation that continues to let him thrive. A child who experiences consistent, dependable care that is responsive to his signals and needs will develop a lasting confidence that his needs will be met, which in turn leads to a trust both in others and in his ability to communicate what he needs.

When evaluating any type of child-care situation, whether one-on-one or group care, consider the following important guidelines.

One caregiver:

- Make sure the caregiver is sensitive to each child's needs and unique individual developmental and cultural characteristics.

- Notice whether the caregiver's interactions with your infant are frequent and of high quality.

- Ensure that the caregiver responds to both verbal and physical signals from your baby.

A home, institutional, or other group day care situation:

- Check to see if the caregivers have attended courses, workshops, or staff development programs.

- Be satisfied that the staff can bond strongly with your child.

- Look for small groups of children.

- Ensure that there is a primary caregiver assigned to infants and toddlers.

- Look for scheduling that keeps a child with an assigned caregiver for as long a period as possible. Children attach most securely to a person who gives them companionship and stimulation on a regular basis—not simply to the person who meets only their physical needs. Make sure your baby gets a chance to really get to know the caregiver who is looking after her.

- Ask about staff turnover; it should be low.

- Be an active, participating parent.

Should you be worried when your baby does attach to her caregiver? Absolutely not. In fact, a 1991 study from the University of Minnesota Center for Early Education and Development, which reported on attachment and bonding, showed that children with secure early attachments are more likely in later years to:

- be better problem solvers
- form friendships and be leaders
- be more empathetic and less aggressive
- engage the world with their confidence
- have higher self-esteem
- be better at resolving conflict
- be more self-reliant and adaptable

If you choose to or have to go back to work, base your child-care decisions on what you have learned about your baby in these early months. When you are able to make knowledgeable decisions about child-care situations, you can return to work—confident that your child will continue to thrive. And, of course, there is plenty of time during the day—before you go to work, and once you have returned home—when you can focus exclusively on your baby, giving her the kind of stimulation she most enjoys and playing the games you have both come to anticipate and enjoy.

BABY TALK

From the beginning of the fourth month to the end of the sixth month, you can expect to see a leap in your baby's language development. Action and response games take on new weight as your baby engages in meaningful two-way communication with you. At first her responses will simply be a gleeful smile or a wriggle of delight. Soon she will be mimicking sounds back to you. Pay attention to how your baby responds to your overtures. When you are talking to your baby, make sure you face her and look at her face for her response. She will learn that her expression will lead you to continue the conversation. My daughter loved a game called " 'Round and 'Round the Garden" (see below) when she was about five or six months old. When I got to the part that immediately preceded the tickle under her chin, she would tense with excitement, her eyes wide with anticipation. Sometimes she would even burst out laughing before the tickle. I loved seeing how she learned what was coming next, her expectant gaze on mine as she waited for her favorite part of the game.

As your baby goes into his sixth month, you will notice that his comprehension is beginning to sharpen. He may recognize names (Mommy, Daddy, those of siblings) and basic words such as "no," "bye-bye," or "bottle." Your baby begins to attach meaning to words through repetition. So although you may not feel like saying "bye-bye" to the dog every time you leave the house, it's a good idea to do so. Adding a wave helps by connecting a gesture to the word.

By the same token, showing and telling become important ways to emphasize language. Use single words as you show baby common items. For instance, when changing your baby, hold up the diaper and tell him, "Diaper. Let's change your diaper." At lunchtime, show him the spoon and say, "Spoon. We eat lunch with a spoon." Allow your baby time to process each concept as you introduce it.

While you may get tired of repeating yourself, rest assured that your baby can't get enough of the same words, stories, or songs. Have a few favorites that you can use consistently. Whether it's "Twinkle, Twinkle, Little Star" or "Itsy-Bitsy Spider" or traditional nursery rhymes like "Hey Diddle Diddle" or "Humpty Dumpty," rhyme and repetition help your baby develop an ear for the rhythm of speech and the flow of words. If you have any doubts about the power of this approach, I can tell you that one mother of a now nine-year-old girl recently told me that her daughter still recites *The Cat in the Hat* from memory. Not surprisingly, it had been one of her favorite stories as a baby.

Your baby is also discovering how to use his developing language skills to be sociable. Unfortunately, your little chatterbox does not possess the skill of volume control at this point! Be prepared for full-volume displays of his whole repertoire of laughs, squeals, and babbling—even at inopportune times.

Books remain a great source of stimulation for your baby at this age. They can also provide you with opportunities to allow your baby to practice nonverbal response. When looking at a picture book, ask your baby questions like "Where's the kitty?" (or doggie, or baby, or Mommy, etc.). Pause and give her a chance to respond. At first she may glance expectantly at you, waiting for you to answer. Soon, she will begin to connect the word "kitty" with the picture on the page and will direct her gaze to the book. One day, no doubt to your surprise and pride, she will touch the book, placing her little finger right on the picture of the kitten.

GAMES

Classic Rhythm and Rhyme

There are many rhyming games you can play with your baby that combine hand movements or touch with short, rhythmic sentences. Here are a few of my favorites:

'Round and 'Round the Garden: *'Round and 'round the garden, goes the teddy bear* (rub your hand in a circular motion on your baby's tummy). *One step, two steps* (slowly walk two fingers up from baby's tummy to chest, pause dramatically, and then swoop in for the last line). *Tickle me under there!* (tickle your baby under her chin).

This Little Piggy: *This little piggy went to market* (wiggle baby's big toe). *This little piggy stayed home* (wiggle second toe). *This little piggy had roast beef* (wiggle third toe). *And this little piggy had none* (wiggle fourth toe). *And this little piggy* (hold pinky toe) *cried "weee weee weee" all the way home* (run your fingers up baby's legs and end with a gentle tickle).

Try varying the game by changing words or skipping a toe and see if your baby notices.

Pop Goes the Weasel: Have your baby sit on your knees, facing you, to play this game. Hold her securely under the arms until she has mastered sitting unsupported—then you can hold her by the hands or wrists for more excitement.

Gently bounce your knees as you sing: *All around the mulberry bush, the monkey chased the weasel. The monkey thought it was all in fun* . . . (pause, and then give a big bump with your knees as you sing) *POP! goes the weasel.*

Make sure you pause before the big bounce and "POP!" so your baby can anticipate what is coming. Once she knows the song, she may try to pop herself up—or even vocalize to "POP!" along with you.

Farmyard Fun

Animal sounds are a big hit with babies in this age group. When you point out a particular animal to your baby—in a book, on the street, in your home—make the corresponding sound and encourage your baby when he makes similar sounds. *Moo, Baa, La La La* by Sandra Boynton is a great book to use when introducing this concept.

Teddy Bear Tête-à-tête

Help your child develop language and social skills at the same time by using his favorite stuffed toys or plush puppets to carry on conversations. You can have the plush playmates talk to each other, to your baby, and to you. Change the pitch and intonation of your voice for each character. If you're fluent in a second language, perhaps "Señor Gato" or "Mademoiselle Chat" can help you to begin to introduce words and phrases. (For more on bilingual babies, see the next chapter for ages seven through nine months.)

THE LITTLE THINGS: FINE MOTOR SKILLS

During the early part of this time period, your baby is still working on gross motor skills. As she gradually begins to master the movement of her arms, torso, and legs, she'll

Bookshelf

Your baby may be starting to become more interested in sharing a "reading" experience with you. Most babies of this age enjoy looking at realistic pictures, especially of family members. Remember that your baby still considers all books fair game for tasting and tugging, so no first editions just yet! Following are some of my favorite reading materials for four- through six-month-olds:

- plastic/vinyl books for bath time
- a small photo album with family and pet pictures
- fabric books that are washable for cuddling and chewing
- *Clap Hands* by Helen Oxenbury
- *That's Not My Puppy* . . . by Fiona Watt and Rachel Wells
- *Pat the Bunny* by Dorothy Kunhardt
- *Moo, Baa, La La La* by Sandra Boynton

begin to refine her ability to use her hands. By four months your baby will swipe at things that interest her. Swiping will quickly turn into grabbing. Your baby will enjoy grabbing on to any object you hand her. If her hands are clenched into fists, try offering her objects by touching them to the back of her hand. But it won't be long before she is reaching for things with an open palm and figuring out how to grab on to them. Babies at this age will enjoy handling most objects you offer to them—and many you don't (like your earrings, hair, nose, etc.). Finally, she'll move on to picking items up with her forefinger and thumb in what is called a pincer grasp.

Make sure your baby has a wide range of things to practice grabbing on to. Squishy throw pillows in different fabrics and textures are easy to grab; small plastic containers filled with objects like beans or marbles or paper clips make noises and shift balance as they are handled (see cautionary note below if using objects with small parts); small plush toys have different parts to grab and explore (look for ones that have bells or rattles inside); different types of paper are visually interesting and make sounds when crumpled.

An Important Note of Caution: I see nothing wrong with letting your baby play with common household items but you must be *very careful* to ensure his safety. Remember that, at this age, your baby explores with his mouth as much as his hands! Be sure that lids on containers are tightly sealed if small objects are inside, or use empty plastic medicine bottles with childproof caps. Make sure that containers are clean and free of paper labels that might be gummed off. Avoid using containers or items that held or contain toxic paints or other dangerous substances, and be sure nothing has sharp edges. Unless you are completely sure you're offering your baby a totally child-safe toy, do not let your baby out of your sight or reach! Instead, join your baby in his exploration of these fascinating household items.

GAMES

Patty-cake and Clap Hands

Any games that draw your baby's attention to his hands are good at this stage. Demonstrate by clapping your own hands, then hold your baby's hands and guide them through the finger play as you sing along. You'll be surprised at how fast he catches on.

The Cup Clutch

Your baby may already be able to curl her hands around a bottle and help support it. Now let her explore how her fingers can work to clutch the rim of a small plastic cup or Tupperware container. Put the cup or container down on a flat surface in front of her and watch as she figures out how to pick it up by grabbing it along the edge.

Chomping Cheerios

By six months your baby will probably enjoy munching on pieces of cereal. Let him practice his pincer skills by putting a few pieces of cereal on a tray in front of him. It's unimportant whether he actually eats the cereal. The task of picking up small items is what's important. But remember, since your baby also explores *everything* by putting it in his mouth, you should be sure that you offer him something that is safe to eat and monitor him closely so that you know he is swallowing safely.

Toy Chest

During these few months, common household objects can offer your baby plenty of opportunity for entertainment and exploration. Remember to offer only one or two choices at a time. Don't overwhelm your little one with too many options. Some good items to have on hand for improvisational toys are:

- wooden spoons
- plastic dishes
- plastic containers with tight lids (fill them with objects that make interesting sounds securely sealed into the container)

Your baby will also enjoy playing with:

- balls
- simple rolling toys
- easy-to-grasp plush animals

If you just can't stay out of the toy stores and know that you're going to make at least one purchase for your baby at this age, I'd recommend getting one of the many kinds of activity tables that are available. These usually have a cloth seat that is surrounded by a plastic tray with different moving toys attached. Sometimes the seat spins around; on some models you can fold down legs to make the table stationary or fold them up under the rounded base to let the whole unit rock from side to side. Your baby can practice standing, spinning, and rocking and will enjoy making all the moving parts of the toys whirl, sway, and jingle. This toy will last well into the next few months and is a great way to keep busy little bodies occupied but safely in one place!

Safety Watch: Toys and Playthings

Childproofing your baby's environment becomes more and more extensive as she grows. In the next chapter I talk about some of the things you need to do to help keep your baby safe once she begins crawling. Right now, as you begin to introduce a variety of toys and objects to your child for her to handle, you need to evaluate the safety of each item. For instance, you should never, ever allow your baby to play with plastic bags of any type. As you consider what household items might make an intriguing toy for your intrepid explorer, consider the following:

- Can this item break?
- Are there sharp edges?
- Is it too heavy?
- Will it be toxic if eaten, licked, or gnawed?
- Does this object contain items that are a choking hazard?

One final note: Some toys or containers may hold items that could be a choking hazard for your child. If you choose to let your child play with such a toy (a paper plate maraca filled with dried beans, for example), make sure you stay with her while she is handling the object, so you can step in and redirect her attention if you need to take the toy from her for safety reasons.

HOW IT ALL FITS: SPATIAL DEVELOPMENT

This period is the beginning of real coordination and purposeful movement for your baby. He now realizes that he can reach toward an object that interests him and can touch it to cause a reaction. As his gross motor control progresses, he will become even more aware of how to move and affect his environment.

He is also becoming aware that there is a relation between visual, auditory, and sensory input. At this stage, he will love to play games that involve giving and taking, like the *Hot Potato* game listed below.

GAMES

Counting Cars

Most infants love to watch passing traffic. If you live on a well-traveled road, pull up a seat at a window with a good view of the road and settle in. If your street is quiet, a visit to a local café or park might be a good way to watch traffic. As you hear a car approaching, call his attention to the sound of the motor: "Here comes the car!" Your baby will fix his attention on the vehicle and turn his head to watch it speed out of sight. Soon he will begin to anticipate the arrival of the car when he hears the approach of the engine. Discuss the cars with him as they pass by: "Look, that car is red. There's a truck."

Hot Potato

Pass a tennis ball or a squishy plush ball back and forth. Hand it to your baby and exclaim in delight as she clutches

Dottie Says

"Mommy loves to take me out visiting. I know she wants to show off how cute and clever I am. In the beginning, I didn't mind meeting all these new people. The truth is, it was kind of a blur. But now! Well, it's sort of scary. Just the other day, some lady calling herself "Auntie" tried to pull me out of Mommy's arms. Who is this lady and why is she taking me away? She looked so different from Mommy that it made me cry."

Around six months, your baby may develop what is commonly referred to as "stranger anxiety." Up until now, you may have had the kind of baby that you could hand off to anyone, anywhere without a peep. And suddenly, even Grandma's smiling face can cause an outburst. Your baby is simply trying to deal with too many new and unfamiliar stimuli.

Now that his awareness of his environment is heightened, he needs time to process each of these stimuli—from a distance. Help him find his comfort zone by asking people he doesn't see regularly to let him study them from a distance before they swoop in to touch or hold him. And though it takes the tact of an international diplomat, ask family to be respectful of his need for a little space at first, especially if it's been a while since he has seen them.

Most important, don't worry about this perfectly normal developmental phase and remind your friends and relatives that it's nothing personal.

it to her. Hold out your hands with an expectant look and see if she will pass the ball to you. In no time at all she'll catch on to the game and squeal with delight when you pass her the ball.

GET UP AND GO: GROSS MOTOR SKILLS

Your baby is on the threshold of real independent movement. He can already roll over, prop himself up on his arms when lying on his belly, and sit up when propped. It's only a matter of time before he learns how to push himself up to sit, creep, or crawl and maybe even pull himself up to stand.

As he begins to challenge himself physically, his vestibular system (a nerve system centered in the brain stem and linked very closely with the cerebellum and inner-ear mechanism) is developing and allowing him to discover new things about balance and coordination. In your baby's early months, you have helped to stimulate the development of this system, although probably unconsciously. Every time you rocked, carried, or swayed your baby in your arms, you were stimulating this developing system.

According to scientists, the vestibular system is one of the first parts of the brain to begin to function after conception. Dr. Richard M. Restak, author of *The Brain: The Last Frontier* and *The Infant Mind*, cites evidence accumulated in recent years that points to early vestibular stimulation as crucial in normal brain development. Rocking, jiggling, and moving rhythmically all stimulate the

Exercising with Your Baby

Your baby is experiencing the exciting notion that his body is under his control. And now that you're a few months postpartum, you may be wishing your body would be back under your control! Exercises that you and your baby can do together are great for enhancing his gross motor development and easing yourself back into shape. Start these simple exercises early and gain strength as your baby gains weight.

Baby bench press. Tones your biceps, upper chest, and shoulders. Lie on your back with your knees bent and feet flat. Place your baby facedown on your chest with your hands supporting him under his arms. Slowly raise your baby off your chest until your arms are fully extended. Slowly lower baby back down to your chest.

The butt bounce. Tones your hips, waist, and buttocks. Sit on the floor with your legs extended. Sit your baby on your lap, with your hands supporting his back and shoulders. "Walk" forward on your buttocks, twisting your torso as you go.

vestibular system. Infants who are stimulated by rocking have been shown to gain weight faster, develop vision and hearing earlier, and demonstrate distinct sleep cycles at an earlier age.

Another study, by Dr. Ruth Rice of Texas, has shown that fifteen minutes, four times a day, of rocking, rubbing, rolling, and stroking a premature baby will greatly enhance that baby's ability to coordinate movement. She makes a further link to cognitive development and the ability to learn.

Rock and roll. Tones your abdominals and strengthens your back. Lie on your back with your knees bent and your lower legs held in the air parallel to the floor. Let your baby lie facedown on your shins with his armpits just over your knees. Support him under the arms. Tucking your chin, slowly raise your head and shoulders and rock forward, curling up as your toes touch the floor. Hold for a minute, and then gently roll back, lowering your head to the floor and bringing your lower legs back to parallel.

Peekaboo sit-ups. Tones your abdominals. Sit on the floor with your knees bent and feet flat on the floor. Rest your baby on his back on your thighs. Hold his hands or wrists. Keeping your lower body still, gently roll back until your back is flat on the floor. Ask your baby, "Where's Mommy?" Roll back up and say "Peekaboo!" Don't forget to breathe during this exercise. To make it more challenging, roll halfway up and hold for 30 seconds, before coming all the way up. Bonus: Letting your baby coax you into a giggling fit during this exercise works your abdominals twice as much!

Your baby will still enjoy being rocked. And if he enjoys it, you can add other movements, such as spinning or dipping or swooping from side to side.

It's important to let your baby learn about her developing motor skills and coordination by letting her try as much as she wants. Allow her space to try to creep. Of course, along with this desire for more movement comes a certain amount of frustration. But don't be too quick to jump in and move your baby if she isn't getting where she wants to be as quickly as she wants to. Babies learn by

Did You Know?: The Vestibular System

The vestibular system refers to the receptors located in the inner ears. Semicircular canals on either side of the inner ear form arches in three different planes that are able to register movement of the head in any direction. It allows us to perceive weight and the effects of gravity.

But the vestibular system is also very closely related to the entire physiology of our bodies. Overstimulation, particularly of the visual system, can provoke motion sickness, which can be thought of as the vestibular system signaling to the digestive system that something is wrong.

The vestibular system also strongly influences muscle tone, communicating to the muscles how much they need to counteract the downward pull of gravity. This comes into play each time we perform an activity requiring balance or expend physical effort to climb stairs, adjust to changing levels (as when riding in an elevator), or recover our balance when we step in a hole.

Vestibular sensations contribute to the development of the nervous system before birth. The fetus's activity, which is sensed by this system, contributes to brain development during gestation.

For infants, turning over, being held upright, or being rocked or carried provides necessary vestibular stimulation. As your child grows, she provides herself with all the stimulation she needs: running, jumping, swinging, turning somersaults, or walking on a balance beam.

doing, and frustration can play an important role in moti-
vating your child to develop the skills that allow her access
to the things she wants.

One of the most frustrating steps in the development of
movement is the fact that a baby who wants to creep forward
often ends up moving backward instead. Your baby may become incredibly frustrated the first few times she tries to
move toward an object and discovers herself scooting farther
away from it instead. You can help her to discover forward
movement by letting her push off with her feet against the
palms of your hands when she is on her stomach.

Of course it's a good idea to have a few diversionary
tactics up your sleeve, since your baby's constant quest for
independent motion can mean a lot of wriggling, rolling,
and slithering—often at inopportune times, like during a
diaper change or in the bath! When you need your baby to
stay still for a few minutes, make sure you give her something else to do by offering visual stimulation. Hang pictures or tape shiny, interesting paper to the wall near her
changing table. Offer easy-to-grip bath toys in the tub.
Make sure your baby doesn't come to consider the necessary pit stops as roadblocks on her path to locomotion.

GAMES

Surfin' Safari

By about five months, most babies love supported standing. Let your baby stand on your knees as you hold her
wrists for balance. As she becomes more secure on her feet,
slowly move your knees from side to side and let her fol-

low the motion. As she finds her balance, you can vary the ride by lifting one knee higher than the other or by gently bouncing both knees in varying rhythms.

Stand Up, Sit Down

While he's in a seated position, let your baby grasp your fingers. Depending on how much support he needs, you can close your hands around his wrists or upper arms. Gently pull him up, letting him bear as much weight on his legs as he wants to. Continue to support him as he folds back into a sitting position.

Thrill Ride

Hold your baby firmly under her arms as you slowly spin in a circle. Let her legs fly out behind her. Vary your spinning speed and raise and lower her as you turn. Don't get so dizzy that you lose your balance! Watch your baby's face carefully as you play this game. She should be smiling or laughing, not looking worried. If she doesn't enjoy this kind of thrill just yet, you can hold her in your arms as if to rock her and try some gentle spins or side-to-side swoops.

chapter five

Get Up and Go:
Seven through Nine Months

As a second-time parent, you often think you've seen it all. You're confident that with your second child, you know exactly what's supposed to come next and when. Our first daughter didn't crawl until she was a little over nine months old. My husband and I waited patiently every day for weeks, wondering when she'd achieve that milestone. Once she did, we figured we knew the timetable for crawling. So of course we confidently predicted that our second daughter would learn to crawl on the same schedule.

One day, when our second daughter was six months old, I noticed she had scooched herself up onto her hands and knees. She was rocking back and forth, as if she was going to take off and go. As an experienced parent, I knew she couldn't be ready to crawl yet; she would crawl when she was nine months old—like her sister did. Imagine my shock when suddenly she just took off! From *that day on, my smug confidence was gone. This second baby was a whirlwind who loved getting into everything she could.*

Amy, Katherine and Taylor's mom

A WHOLE NEW WORLD

Over these next three months, you can expect to see your baby's mastery of her developing skills kick into a whole new gear. You will really be able to appreciate how the stimulation you have provided her with since she was a newborn pays off. For example, the hours you have spent rocking your baby and stimulating her gross motor control will allow her to sit unsupported, and then to act upon her increasing desire to crawl. Most parents find this a particularly fulfilling time in their baby's development. It is very rewarding to see the ways in which your stimulation and interaction help shape your child into a confident, happy, and curious baby who is able to quickly process the input from all her senses as she explores her world.

HERE, THERE, AND EVERYWHERE

The beginning of your baby's seventh month marks the beginning of a very physical half year. Your baby is learning to sit up on her own; to get around on her own by creeping, scooting, or crawling; and to balance herself on her feet. All of these skills require a great deal of physical effort on your baby's part, and you will see her practicing them endlessly. She is ready to control the body that she has previously worked so hard to command. If you have a very physically active baby, I can promise you that your days of attending to various grown-up chores as your baby sits propped up and watching are over. Get ready to ratchet up your own physical level of activity as you keep up with your newly mobile, endlessly curious little whirlwind.

But don't think these three months are only about action. Even as your baby works to advance his mobility, he is changing in an amazing number of other ways. He has now discovered that he can use his hands to explore things by means other than grabbing them and moving them to his mouth. He can now touch, pat, and stroke, allowing him to explore the surfaces of items too big to grasp. Texture becomes much more interesting to your baby as he begins to understand that he can learn about things through sensation. Dropping things becomes an endlessly fascinating game as he learns that he can clasp and unclasp his fingers.

Your baby's speech and language capacity is also developing rapidly during this period. She begins to comprehend that the babbling sounds she makes can be social overtures. Babies at this age enjoy "conversations" immensely, and your response to their babbled conversation is a crucial part of early language stimulation. Your baby is also learning to connect words to objects. That's right. You didn't just imagine that she looked at her stroller when you said "go for a walk." Or looked right at her father when someone said "Daddy."

Your baby is also working on communicating with you on a more sophisticated emotional level. His crying can signal unhappiness or frustration or rage or fear. Just as it was important to understand what your baby's earliest cries signaled, it is now important to be attuned to what he is telling you when he dissolves into tears. Other emotional developments manifest themselves in an increase of stranger anxiety or sleep disturbances. In this chapter I offer some hints for dealing with these new and often intense feelings.

Your baby is at an exciting developmental stage as she gains control and mobility over these three months. How you respond to her ceaseless need to discover all she can about the larger world that has opened up to her is vitally important to her growth as a smarter, happier baby. Think back to the earlier chapters of this book and the logical way in which your baby has progressed. And how your earliest stimulation has led naturally to this point. Simply by interacting with your baby in a nurturing and responsive way, you've given her the tools she needs to acquire new skills. As she moves through this next developmental stage, remember that babies grow in patterns. From birth they are programmed to be explorers. And it's your job to provide a safe, encouraging environment for their explorations.

SLEEPING AND WAKING

The good news is that your baby may finally have settled into a fairly predictable sleep schedule. The bad news is that most babies consolidate their two naps into one longer nap during this time period. Of course, if your baby has always been a good sleeper, the twice-a-day napping

Games Siblings Play

This is a great period for older children. Their baby sibling can now move around enough to play some interactive, physical games but is not so mobile that she can get into all her big brother's or sister's toys. Enjoy this brief moment of peace in your household! Here are some games that are perfect for a crawling baby and her bigger siblings.

- **Follow the Leader.** Let the older sibling take the lead as he or she encourages the baby to follow on a (safe) obstacle course around furniture, under tables, and over pillows that have been strewn on the floor.

- **Chase Me.** Reverse the situation and let the baby take the lead as his brother or sister follows him around. "Gonna getcha" is the heralding cry of this game as the bigger child manages to grab a tiny toe or ankle before allowing the baby to break free. Be sure to caution the older sibling not to tackle the younger too hard, and watch the first few games to be sure the older child understands that baby isn't indestructible.

- **Catch or Fetch.** Perfect for babies who can only sit, and easily modified for those who are crawling. Have your older child and baby sit facing each other and gently roll a ball back and forth.

may persist into his second year. As long as your baby's nighttime quality of sleep is good, don't worry about how much—or how little—sleep your baby requires during daylight hours.

Ensuring a good night's sleep for your baby may require a little more effort right now, mainly because your baby has learned to keep himself awake. If you haven't experienced any sleep difficulties with your baby in the past, don't panic if they surface during these next few months. Whereas in the past he would simply doze off uncontrollably whenever he needed rest, these days excitement, tension, or simply an unwillingness to miss out on any of the action around him can keep him awake well past a reasonable bedtime.

If you are struggling with your baby's sleeping patterns, there are many child-care books that suggest various techniques for helping babies to fall—and stay—asleep. I don't have a particular program to ensure that your baby sleeps well, but I can offer these few simple steps that worked with my kids and may help prime your baby for a good night's sleep. It's been my experience that a baby who learns to welcome nighttime sleep now is well on the way to being a child who obediently trots off to bed when he is older.

Relaxing bedtime routines:

* **A warm bath.** Your crawling baby is probably dirty by the end of the day anyway. Use the sleep-inducing powers of a warm soothing bath to set a bedtime mood.

* **A sleepy atmosphere.** Dim lights, quiet, and a minimum of outside distractions will encourage relaxation and sleep.

* **A song or a story:** Spend some time cuddling your baby while singing or reading. Gently rock and listen to a favorite CD of soothing songs or classical music. (At our house, music always resulted in a relaxed and drowsy state—often for me as well as my daughters—so we gathered some of our favorites onto the Baby Prodigy *Musical Pacifier* CDs. You can use ours or make your favorite mix.) It's important to let baby wind down after a busy day of learning.

* **Tucking everybody in.** Make sure your baby has her favorite cuddly or comfort object. Put a favorite animal to bed first, tucking it in and kissing it good night.

* **Banishing any fear of the dark.** If your baby doesn't like total darkness, make sure he has a night-light.

* **See you tomorrow.** Kiss your baby good night and let him know you'll see him in the morning.

Your baby may also be experiencing an increase in night waking. By nine months (or sooner) most babies have given up middle-of-the-night feedings. It is not likely that your baby is waking from hunger. Instead, he may be awakened by loud noises, becoming too cold, an internal disturbance (a dream, perhaps, or something physical like a gas pain or cramp), or teething pain. Believe it or not, babies who do not get enough sleep during the day are often unable to settle into a deep sleep at night and stay there.

Did You Know?: Self-Comforting

As your baby learns to let herself drift off to sleep, she may employ a variety of behaviors to help her relax and unwind. While you may prefer a hot bath and a cup of chamomile tea to help you ease off to dreamland, don't be surprised if your baby chooses any of the following techniques:

- **Sucking.** The most basic of all comforting habits for babies. Your baby may choose to suck his fingers, a pacifier, a toy, or a corner of a blanket. Sucking is often combined with other activities, like pulling on his ears, or twisting his hair. Some babies twist their hair so much that they actually start to pluck it out.

- **Cuddlies.** A blanket, a favorite plush toy, a piece of fabric. Your baby will need this object for comfort and will refuse to relinquish it, even when it becomes worn to a shadow of its former self. If your baby is particularly attached to a particular toy or blanket, buy duplicates and keep them on hand for backups. I can't tell you how awful it is to arrive home after a long trip and unpack, only to find you've left Mr. Bunny back at the hotel.

- **Rhythmical movements.** Rocking, rolling from side to side, or rocking on hands and knees. This may be soothing to some babies. Others may gently bop their head against the mattress or the head of their crib.

If your baby wakes in the night, my advice is to go to her and comfort her by laying your hand on her back and gently rubbing or patting. You can offer her a soothing whisper or just tell her, "Ssshhhhh." Do not turn on lights, pick your baby up, or introduce any stimulation (like music). Often your baby will fall back to sleep the moment she feels your hand on her back. If your baby persists in crying or shows other behavior that concerns you, then by all means make sure that she is not sick or otherwise in pain.

This light sleep, and subsequent restless waking, is common in babies when they are mastering new activities like sitting or crawling, or pulling themselves to a standing position. With an older baby, you may be summoned to his room by a cry, only to find him standing at the rail of his crib. So intent is he on mastering this new skill that he cannot help himself from trying at any opportunity. Unfortunately, until he becomes skilled at letting himself back down, he will stand there stuck, tired, and probably screaming in frustration until you come in and give him a hand.

These brief night wakings will go on for much of your baby's first year. Don't panic, however, at the thought of never having a solid night's sleep of your own. As your baby internalizes some of the self-comforting techniques above, he will learn to put himself back to sleep from these episodes of waking.

STIMULATING YOUR BABY

As your baby spends more and more time wakeful and engaged with the world around him, your opportunities for providing positive stimulation increase. From the seventh through ninth months, you can help your baby become

Alarm Clock Trick

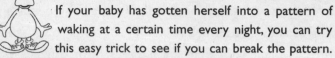

If your baby has gotten herself into a pattern of waking at a certain time every night, you can try this easy trick to see if you can break the pattern.

Say your baby is waking at 4:00 each morning, bright, cheerful, and ready to begin her day. And say that you, perhaps, would prefer a more civilized 6:00 a.m. wake-up call. Try setting an alarm clock to wake your baby at 3:00 or 3:30. When she wakes up, go in, comfort her, and soothe her back to sleep. Do this for a week, and then don't set any alarms. After a week of resetting your baby's built-in body clock, you may find that she sleeps through her 4:00 a.m. internal alarm and wakes a bit later. If this doesn't correct your problem, then you may have a bona fide early bird—and my deepest sympathies.

smarter and happier by using the time you spend with him to focus on enhancing motor, cognitive, and language development. Simple old-fashioned games and activities are often the best way to do this.

Continue to talk to your baby about what you are doing as you move through the day. Using language in relation to ongoing events is one of the strongest ways to enhance brain development in that area. Be aware that the language exposure your child benefits most from is "live" language. At this age, language as heard on television is perceived as nothing more than noise. Furthermore, experts believe that information embedded in an emotional context affects neural circuitry more powerfully than information alone. This seems to be particularly true when your baby is learning concepts such as "more," as in "Here are *more* Cheerios" as you hand her another bowl, or "later," as in "We'll play with the doll *later;* now we are getting dressed."

Your baby will also be testing and improving his cognitive skills, developing a sense of object permanence (the idea that objects, people, and things are present even when he can't see them) and a sense of herself as an independent individual. Mirrors are appealing to babies at this age, as are games like peekaboo and hiding toys under blankets. Stranger awareness, often accompanied by anxiety, is a natural by-product of these developments.

Motor skills are steadily developing as well. Surmounting repeated frustrations, your baby will practice sitting, standing, and crawling. Each skill he masters allows him more opportunities for exploring and sensory stimulation.

Childproofing takes on a whole new importance once your baby reaches this stage. It is vitally important that you provide your baby with a safe environment so he can have the freedom to explore without danger. For parents, these next few months should be a time of extreme vigilance. Let your baby's growing vocabulary be helpful here. Teach your baby words and phrases like "Don't touch," "Ouch," "Dangerous," "Hot," and "Boo-boo."

BABY STEPS

From the beginning of the seventh month to the end of the ninth month, your baby will begin to discover the ever-expanding range of his coordination. From sitting to

Safety Watch: Babyproofing Your Home

There are many babyproofing kits on the market that can help you to make your home safer for your little explorer. But there are also simple, common-sense steps you can take to make your home safer. Here's a long, but by no means comprehensive, list of babyproofing techniques for your home.

Kitchen

- Install latches on drawers and cabinets that contain items that might harm baby.

- Remove all poisons or toxic materials from under the sink and place them in locations high enough that even a standing baby won't be able to reach them.

- Remove magnets from the refrigerator; if they fall and break, your baby can swallow the magnet. Flat, business card–type magnets are okay, although your baby may gnaw on them once he removes them from the fridge.

- Wash out all bottles of cleaning fluid and other toxic chemicals before throwing them in the trash or recycling bin. Just one drop can be harmful to babies.

Bathroom

- Remove all soaps, razors, and shampoos from the edge of the tub.

- You may want to cover the bathtub spout to protect your baby from bumping her head on it during bath times.

- Put a lock on the toilet lid.

- *Never* leave an infant alone in a tub. Babies can drown in just an inch or two of water.

Baby's Room

- Any types of mirrors, busy boxes, or crib attachments should be installed on the wall side of the crib so your baby can't use them as a stepladder on her way to climbing out of her crib.

- Remove mobiles from the crib.

- Always use the straps on your changing table, and never leave your baby unattended on a surface higher than the floor.

In General

- Cover all electrical outlets, even those behind furniture. It's amazing where those tiny hands can reach.

- Turn your hot water down to 120 degrees to lessen chances of accidental scalding.

- Keep houseplants away from your baby. Some are toxic.

- Move hanging cords from phones, answering machines, and other electronics out of your baby's reach.

- Do not use tacks or staples to secure electrical cords to walls or molding. Duct tape may be unattractive, but your baby is less likely to pull it off the wall and swallow it.

- If you have a brick or stone fireplace, consider installing a bumper pad. Think about putting bumpers around glass coffee tables as well. It's probably best to remove glass coffee tables altogether, as the panes may not support the weight of a baby who manages to climb atop the table.

- Keep your baby away from home exercise equipment. It's easy for small fingers to get pinched or stuck.

- Cords from window blinds or shades should be lifted out of reach or shortened.

- Separate dog or cat food from baby. Your baby could choke on a piece of kibble, or your dog could perceive your baby as stealing its food and snap at him.

- Block off dog or cat doors so your baby does not take to using them as well.

- Put gates up at the top and bottom of stairs.

- Get the number of your local poison control center and tape it up in a visible location as well as by each phone. Program it into your cell phone if appropriate. Keep a bottle of syrup of ipecac in your medicine cabinet, but don't use it unless instructed by your pediatrician or poison control center.

standing, from using bottles to eating finger foods, from crawling to cruising, every activity is an opportunity to explore new frontiers.

By the end of the ninth month, your child should have achieved the milestones listed below. If you are concerned about your child's rate of development, consult your pediatrician.

Sometime between the beginning of the seventh month and the end of the eighth month, your baby should be able to:

* feed herself a cracker
* babble using a combination of vowels and consonants
* say "Mama" or "Dada" (indiscriminately)
* sit without support

* work to get a toy that is out of reach
* pass an object from one hand to the other
* pick up a tiny object in a pincer grip
* push to her hands and knees and rock back and forth
* bear some weight on her legs when supported
* stand, holding on to objects
* pull to a stand from sitting
* "cruise" walk by holding on to furniture
* play patty-cake or wave bye-bye
* play peekaboo

By the end of the ninth month, your baby should be able to:

* understand the meaning of certain words (like "no")
* say "Mama" and "Dada" (with appropriate meaning)
* say other simple words (like "bye")
* drink from a cup
* crawl quickly and with intent
* stand alone, without support
* take a few steps without support (Yikes!)
* respond to a simple command when combined with hand gestures (your saying "Give a hug" with your arms held out)

Your Baby's View

Imagine that you've finally gotten away on your dream vacation—maybe to France or to Greece. You've been on a lovely tour through the streets of the city but are tired and thirsty. You'd love to have a cold drink. There's no café handy, but you see someone not far ahead and hurry to catch up to her. "Where could I get something to drink?" you ask. You are met with a blank stare. The dreaded language barrier looms between the two of you. Thinking quickly, you mime sipping from a cup and are rewarded with a huge smile and hand gestures that direct you just down the street and around the corner, where you find a charming café. *That wasn't so hard,* you think, as you sit down and repeat the sipping gesture while pointing at the coffee cup on the table across from you. *We understood each other perfectly.*

Simple sign language can help your baby as she turns her babbled "foreign" speech into recognizable English. By about eight months, babies usually have sufficient motor coordination to begin to make simple signs and gestures to communicate basic needs. Recent research in neuroscience has shown that there is significant overlap between the areas of the brain that control the mouth and speech and the areas that control the hands and gestures. These areas are thought to develop in tandem, with progress in one area enhancing ability in the other. If you are interested in trying sign language with your baby, see the Bookshelf section in this chapter for a few titles that will help you to learn more.

BABY TALK

Your baby is at an important developmental stage regarding language. But what's important is not that he learns to say particular words or even mimic speech by parroting words back, but that he begin to understand what words mean and how they relate to things. At this age, your baby needs to have plenty of opportunities to listen to conversation, the chance to grasp the meanings of the words he recognizes, and a positive social response when he attempts to join the conversation.

If you think about it, you've become quite accomplished at understanding what your baby needs or wants over the last few months. In fact, she's been able to communicate her needs very clearly. And she's beginning to understand you as well. Before a baby can speak, she understands dozens of words. When you say, "Let's put your shoes on," and your baby crawls over to her shoes, it's not just a coincidence. Be sure to label items, taking care not to refer simply to "them" or "it." Asking your baby "Where is the ball?" as you search the room will make a stronger connection than saying "Where is it?"

What you'll notice over these next few months is the pleasure your baby takes in using sounds, and then syllables that sound like words, to express herself. You will hear lots of babbling as your baby tries out sounds, tones, volume, and conversational rhythms that please her.

If you speak a second language and would like your baby to be bilingual as well, this is a good time to begin. If one parent speaks a second language, that parent should primarily use that language when speaking to the baby. The other parent should use the language he or she is most comfortable speaking in.

Continue to make reading a daily part of your baby's routine and set an example by letting your baby see you read. Show them "Mommy's (or Daddy's) books." Reading to your baby should be an interactive experience. Take time to point out items of interest on the page and be prepared to revisit favorite books and pages over and over again.

GAMES

Everything Has a Name

Take your baby for a walk around the house or the neighborhood, pointing out objects as you go. Repeat words often and make sure that your baby is looking at the objects as you name them. Pay attention to what interests your baby. If you are walking outside, and she hears a dog barking and looks around, help her to find the dog. Once she has located it visually you can tell her: "There's Mr. Smith's *dog*. The *dog's* name is Blackie. The *dog* says 'woof, woof.'" Remember to positively acknowledge any comments your baby offers.

Sing-along

Songs like "Twinkle, Twinkle, Little Star," or "The Wheels on the Bus" help your baby learn the patterns and intonations of language. Lots of repetitive words allow plenty of chances for your baby to chime in with similar sounds.

Bookshelf

Your baby is able to recognize certain pictures and to indicate which pictures she would like to look at. Board books remain the best choice, as the interest in exploring the paper pages of an illustrated book may result in rips. Exploration of books shouldn't be discouraged, however. Keep a supply of back issues of glossy magazines full of colorful pages on hand. Your baby will enjoy turning pages, crumpling sheets, and generally using the magazine for her own purposes.

Books for You

As I mentioned above, there are several books that tell you how to teach your baby to use infant sign language. Here are a sampling of the many that are available:

- *Baby Fingers: Teaching Your Baby to Sign* by Lora Heller
- *Baby Sign Language Basics* by Monta Z. Briant
- *The Baby Signs* series by Linda Acredolo, Ph.D., and Susan Goodwyn, Ph.D.
- *Baby's First Signs* by Kim Votry and Curt Waller

Books to Enjoy with Your Baby

Books you read to your baby now will likely continue to be favorites well into their second year. Make sure you choose books you enjoy, as you will be reading them over and over again in the coming months! Some of my favorites include:

- *Read-Aloud Rhymes for the Very Young* by Jack Prelutsky, illustrated by Marc Brown
- *Let's Try* by Amy MacDonald and Maureen Roffey
- *Babies Start Here* by Bill Gillham and Liz Pichon
- *I See* by Helen Oxenbury

Dookie Says

"Eating has become so much more interesting now that I can put the food in my mouth all by myself. Everything feels so different. In fact, a lot of the time, I never even get around to eating what Daddy gives me because it's just so much more fun to squish, smear, smash, and poke at whatever he's offering."

The development of the pincer grasp opens new frontiers in the dining experience for you and your baby. At this age, your baby is able to effectively gum a wide variety of foods, and you can incorporate lots of new tastes and textures into his diet. Start with foods that are mushy, with a texture just slightly more coarse than puréed baby foods, and move on to manageable sizes of foods that are easily gummed to a consistency that is easy to swallow or that melt in the mouth. Firmer items should be small enough that they don't pose a choking hazard, and softer foods can be slightly larger. If your baby has food allergies or is sensitive to some foods, follow your pediatrician's advice for introducing new foods. And remember, these foods are not meant to meet your baby's full nutritional needs. Your baby will still be getting breast milk or formula and baby cereal. At this age, these food choices are strictly to introduce your baby to the *concept* of other foods and self-feeding. Most babies will enjoy some or all of the following:

- whole wheat bagels, bread, or crackers
- unsalted rice cakes

- easy to grab O-shaped cereal (without added salt or sugar)
- puffed rice, corn, or wheat cereal
- cheese such as Edam, Gouda, baby Swiss, or Havarti
- chunks of fruit such as banana (very ripe and soft), pear, mango, peach, or melon
- vegetables (cooked until very tender) such as carrots, broccoli (florets only), mashed peas, or sweet potatoes
- pasta of various sizes and shapes
- scrambled egg yolk

Do not offer your baby foods that are a choking hazard or can be sucked into the windpipe, including:

- whole grapes
- raisins
- popcorn
- nuts
- whole peas
- raw vegetables
- hard fruits (apples, unripe pears)
- chunks of chicken or meat, including hot dogs

Once your baby's molars come in toward the end of the first year or the beginning of the second, you may introduce some of these foods, but carefully.

Songs with rhymes will help your baby hear the small differences in sounds. If you don't have an extensive repertoire of baby-friendly tunes, check out the music section at any department store. There are many CDs with songs specifically for children. Be sure that you sing along; it's your interaction with your child that is most beneficial.

Command Performance

Teach your baby any of the adorably classic baby "tricks" and help them link the actions to the words. The positive feedback that your baby will get from both you and equally charmed adults will encourage a positive link between words, actions, and reactions. Some of the simple actions with the highest "*Awwwww*" factors include waving bye-bye, giving a hug, and blowing a kiss.

THE LITTLE THINGS: FINE MOTOR SKILLS

As your baby begins to gain command of his gross motor skills by learning to sit without support, you will notice a parallel development of his fine motor abilities. Once he has more control over his body, his hands become more and more exciting to him. Over the next few months, he will practice picking up objects with his fingers, passing objects from hand to hand, and releasing his grip on objects, allowing them to drop to the floor. It's likely that your baby will still try to further explore all the exciting objects he finds, from carpet fuzz to dog food, by putting them in his mouth. What this means for you is that the time you will gain in your day as your baby learns to amuse himself for brief periods will need to be spent attending to housekeeping! For the next few months it is important to keep your baby's environment cleaner than usual.

The development of the pincer grasp—using the forefinger and thumb to delicately pick up even the smallest of items—means that your baby can practice feeding himself. There are many appropriate foods to let baby experiment with. I suggest some in the box in this section (see pp. 130–131).

During this time, your baby may also begin to show a reliable preference for using one hand or the other. You can help your baby become more competent with her hands by offering a wide variety of items to allow her to experiment with her new skills. Hand her a spoon to hold at suppertime or hand her the washcloth while she's in her bath. You can encourage your baby's growing interest in texture by letting her explore and stroke different surfaces like carpeting, grass, wood or tile, or even family pets.

Be conscious of gesturing when you speak to your baby. Let him watch as you use your hands. Show him how to operate pull toys, using his hands to move the string to bring the toy closer. From now on, your baby is learning how to use objects not only by experimentation, but also by observation.

An Important Note of Caution: As I indicated earlier, I see nothing wrong with letting your baby play with common household items, but you must be *very careful* to ensure his safety. Be sure that lids on containers are tightly sealed if small objects are inside, or use empty plastic medicine bottles with childproof caps. Make sure that containers are clean and free of paper labels that might be gummed off. Avoid using containers or items that held or contain toxic paints or other substances and be sure nothing has sharp edges. Unless you are completely sure you're offering your baby a totally child-safe toy, do not let your baby out of your sight or reach! Instead, join your baby in his exploration of these fascinating household items.

GAMES

Fishing for Toys

Tie pieces of wool yarn to your baby's favorite toy and help her to learn how she can drop or throw the toy and retrieve it by pulling on the yarn. Don't leave your baby alone with any type of toy that has a pull string attached.

Big and Little

Offer your baby similar items of differing size—your sock and his sock, a big ball and a little ball, a tiny plush animal and a larger one of the same type. He will explore how best to grip and hold objects of varying size. Don't forget to explain to him as you do this that some objects are "big" and some are "little." A toy that is ideal for this type of game is the plastic or wooden rings that stack on a spindle. As your baby grows older, he will begin trying to replace the rings on the spindle after he handles them.

Fill 'Em Up

Your baby will become very interested in putting things into containers and taking them out again. Begin with simple, easy-to-grasp items, like small wooden blocks or

Toy Chest

Household items still make the best and most interesting toys for your baby. During these few months, your baby is focused on mastering crawling; finding, grasping, and examining items of varying sizes and textures; developing expectations about what will happen next; and exploring concepts of permanence and cause and effect. All the toys from the previous chapters can be put to use in more sophisticated ways. Here's a list of other age-appropriate toys to jump-start your imagination. I hope it will get you thinking about what other kinds of common items make wonderful toys that allow you to stimulate your baby in all sorts of ways:

- pots and pans with lids
- stacking toys like rings on a spindle or boxes that fit inside one another
- a jack-in-the-box or other pop-up toys
- couch cushions for makeshift obstacle courses
- scarves and pieces of fabric for peekaboo games
- plush toys for comforting and modeling conversations
- toys on strings
- mirrors
- a flashlight (to play spotlight games and create shadows and patterns)
- soap bubbles for catching and chasing
- beanbags
- activity boards or books with a variety of textures, sounds, and parts that move

Teething

Around six months—sometimes earlier—you should discover your baby's first little pearl of a tooth, usually one of the lower incisors. Once you've made this milestone discovery, teeth will begin erupting fast and furiously for the remainder of the year. By about eight months, most babies have their four front teeth on the top as well as two bottom incisors. By the end of the ninth month, you'll probably see four top and four bottom teeth. Molars generally make their appearance sometime around your baby's first birthday.

How can you tell your baby is teething? Well, everyone's experience is different, but in general you can be on the lookout for some or all of the following signs:

- drooling
- a rash on the face or chin (from all the drooling!)
- biting (to produce pressure on the gums)
- pain or discomfort

squishy balls, and a container that has a wide opening (even a simple box without a lid will do). Show your baby how she can pick objects up and put them in the box. Over the next few months, as her dexterity increases, vary the complexity of the shapes and the size of the opening of the container. This game is also fun in the bath. Provide your baby with plastic cups of varying size and demonstrate how to fill them with bathwater, and then pour it out. Be aware that your baby will probably try to bring the cup filled with water to her mouth—most likely with startling results!

- general irritability
- a temporary loss of interest in feeding or nursing
- ear pulling or the rubbing of cheeks or mouth
- chewing, chewing, chewing (on anything and everything)

For some babies, cutting teeth seems to be a breeze. Others have a harder time of it. If your baby seems very uncomfortable, there are a few different remedies you can try to ease teething pain and pressure. Experiment and see what brings your baby the most comfort as you wait for those new teeth to break through.

- Over-the-counter pain-relief medications may help soothe your baby through the worst of her teething pains.
- Try offering her cold, hard things to bite on. Most baby stores sell special teething toys that can be stored in the freezer and used for icy relief.
- Rub her gums with your finger or a cold washcloth. The counterpressure on her swollen gums may bring relief.

The Mystery Box

Teach your baby about causality and textures at the same time by creating a "mystery box." Cover the open end of a large cardboard box with a piece of fabric with a large hole in the center. Fill the box with a few items of varying textures that are easy to grasp, like scraps of velvet fabric, cotton balls, a plastic spoon, a piece of bark from a tree, a leaf—be imaginative! Show your baby how he can put his hand through the fabric to feel the items, then pull his hand out to more closely examine his prize. (You must not your baby alone with this toy, as he might decide to "try" one of the objects in his mouth. If you are going to leave him alone, be sure items in the box are large enough and nontoxic so as not to prove dangerous if baby should decide to taste them.)

HOW IT ALL FITS: SPATIAL DEVELOPMENT

Your baby is beginning to learn how she and other objects take up space in the world. She will be very interested in games that involve hiding and discovering objects and will probably have a renewed fascination with mirrors and the objects (aside from her own image) that appear in them. Once your baby is crawling, she will explore spatial relations by crawling over, under, or through objects. And when your baby is pulling to a stand or even cruising by the end of the ninth month, she will have added an entirely new dimension to her perception of the world. She is no longer limited to the flat world of crawling along the floor.

The concepts of both object permanence—the knowledge that an object is still present even when he can't see it—and causality—the exploration of how things work or relate—will come to the forefront of your baby's knowledge over the next few months. You may see your baby rolling his ball or pushing his truck across the floor, only to go after it and push it away again. He is not trying to get the truck or ball as much as he is testing his mastery over his space.

Games that allow your baby to explore all of these new relationships between himself and his surroundings will not only be entertaining but will also enhance his confidence and promote his ability to access references, make judgments, and develop expectations of success at various tasks.

GAMES

Bubbles, Tiny Bubbles

Another of our favorite bath time or outdoor games was blowing soap bubbles. Both of my daughters were captivated by the floating bubbles and would reach out, trying to catch them. When they succeeded in touching one, they would laugh in delight as it popped in their hands. This game is particularly fun outdoors, where you can blow bubbles close to the ground and encourage your baby to crawl after them.

Soooo Big

Ask "How big is baby?"—or Kitty, or Daddy, or Brother, or Sister—and help your child to spread his arms as wide as he can while you exclaim "Soooo big!"

Hide-and-Seek

This less-sophisticated version of the classic game involves covering your face, or a toy, or your baby with a cloth or blanket. Ask your baby, "Where's [fill in the blank]?" Pull the cloth or blanket away and exclaim, "There's [fill in the blank]!" or "I see [fill in the blank]!" Before long, your baby will be eagerly reaching out to pull the covering off the hidden object and crowing in delight at his discovery. This version of peekaboo helps to develop your baby's understanding of object permanence, and I guarantee it will be a favorite game.

Is the Glass Half-full or Half-empty?

Use four baby bottles or sippy cups to explore the difference between full and empty. Fill one bottle with water. Pour half into another, add some food coloring to one of the bottles, and then pour the colored water into a third bottle. Mix the colored water with the plain and watch as they turn the same color.

GET UP AND GO: GROSS MOTOR SKILLS

Movement is vitally important for an infant during this time period. The more your baby is allowed to move freely and practice his budding motor skills, the more fine-tuned his motor pathways become and the more adept his developing brain will be at controlling and coordinating the movements necessary for sitting, standing, crawling, and walking.

It's amazing to watch how fast your baby learns to propel herself from one point to another. Much of her movement is motivated by her increasing desire to reach objects of interest. Your baby may follow the common developmental pattern of creeping (wriggling along on her belly), to crawling (moving on hands and knees, on hands and feet, or some combination of those four limbs, including the odd-looking but common "tripod" approach, where one knee is on the floor and one leg sticks straight out to the side for more speed), to cruising (standing and pulling, lurching, or shuffling from one piece of furniture to the next). Or your baby may be a "scooter," one who scoots along on her behind, propelled by her hands. I should warn you that most scooters tend to skip crawling altogether in favor of going straight to walking.

This active stage of babyhood calls for increased vigilance on your part. It's important to remember that your baby needs to learn to sit back down once he's pulled himself to a stand. This can be a trial-and-error process, resulting in more than a few bonks to the head.

The good news is that babies' skulls are specifically designed for this period of rough use. The soft spot (fontanel) on the top of their head is not fully closed, and the flexible nature of their skulls means that a bop to the head may be painful but not always serious. (Of course, if your baby hits his head hard enough to get knocked out or fails to cry right away after a fall, it could be a sign of a concussion. Standing is best practiced barefoot on wood floors or carpeted surfaces.) If your child is a real daredevil and is inclined to hurl himself around with little regard for his noggin, you can buy colorful foam pieces that fit together like a jigsaw puzzle. Use them as moveable floor pads until your child is steady on his feet.

The bad news is that your baby will seem to have his most spectacular bumps and bruises right before a doctor's checkup or a visit from his grandparents! I can remember more than one occasion when I had to bring my younger daughter to family gatherings sporting a spectacular bruise and egg combination on her forehead. So do all you can to keep your baby safe until she is confident in her balance. Remove her socks on slippery wooden or tile floors, do not let her practice standing at the edge of the bathtub—or anywhere in the bathroom (trust me on this one!)—and avoid baby shoes indoors so she can use her toes to grip the ground as she learns to balance.

In these few months, your baby is working toward mastering an incredibly complex set of skills, and you can expect this undertaking to occupy her day and night. Sitting and creeping render anything higher than the floor a new danger zone. Crawling lets your baby explore all corners of your home, and forces you to consider your housekeeping standards and furniture placement. Crib bars make excellent supports for standing, and it's likely your baby will decide that bedtime is as good a time as any to work on her new skill. Unfortunately, once she's standing in her crib, she may realize that the padded crib bumper also makes an excellent stepping-stone. If you don't want her figuring out how to get up and out of the crib just yet, better remove the bumpers now.

Don't let these new challenges frustrate you or cause you to limit your baby's freedom to move and explore on his own. Gates, baby-proofing kits, and constant vigilance are your best investments in maintaining your own peace of mind as your baby makes his way through this key developmental period.

GAMES

She'll Be Coming 'Round the Mountain

Pile up cushions or pillows to make a climbing mountain. Make sure there is adequate padding on all sides of the base of your mountain. Create a tunnel out of a blanket draped over two chairs. Tip large, clean cardboard boxes on their sides. Encourage your baby to crawl up, over, into, through, and around.

In the Spotlight

Use a flashlight to illuminate toys or different spots in a room. Your baby should crawl toward the lit objects. Once he has the hang of the game, point the flashlight at the floor and let him chase the circle of light from its beam.

Stand Up, Sit Down

Kneel facing your baby, holding his hands in yours. Sit down on the back of your legs while your baby sits on the floor. Say, "Stand up" as you pop up to your knees. Help your baby as he stiffens his legs and rises to standing. Say, "Sit down," and lower yourself down again. Keep your baby supported as he figures out how to plop down on his diaper-cushioned behind. Repeat until your knees can't take it anymore.

Dance Party

Play up-tempo music for a rockin' dance party as you help your baby learn to "dance" on her own. Begin by holding her by the waist and gently bouncing her up and down as she kicks her legs to the music. As she becomes steadier on her feet, hold her under the arms and let her bounce on her legs. When she is standing with confidence, you can hold her hands and let her bounce herself. Throw in special effects via a glittering disco ball and have a blast!

Dottie Says

"I can't believe all the things I can do now. I can move to wherever I want. No one needs to carry me for me to be able to look at things. And there are so many interesting things down here. And I get all sorts of new things on my lunch tray. Some are tasty, but others make very excellent pastes and creams. I love to smoosh things between my hands. Can I help it if I get an itchy head right in the middle of squashing up some cottage cheese or eating applesauce, and I have to scratch the itch? But Mommy's driving me crazy—she's always swiping at my face with a cloth or grabbing my hands and washing them off. When I'm wearing the pretty outfits from Grandma, all I hear is 'Don't crawl in that dirt!' How am I supposed to get anything done when I have to get wiped down all the time?"

Sad, but true: That little doll you were able to dress in sweet outfits is now a grime-accumulating, dust-and-dirt magnet that may rival Pigpen from the Charlie Brown gang. But too much focus on keeping your baby spotless can inhibit her from the necessary explorations that will help her to refine and expand her new skills. So when you see your baby heading toward that slightly muddy patch in the garden, take a deep breath and remind yourself that she's entirely washable—and so are her clothes!

chapter six

First Steps:
Ten through Twelve Months

One of the most exciting days in my life was watching our daughter take her first steps. Even though she'd been showing signs she was ready to walk, it still caught me completely off guard. I was in the kitchen, starting dinner one night, and turned around to get a pot out of the cabinet, and there was Megan, taking her first steps toward me! I'll never forget her little hands waving in the air back and forth to balance herself as she tottered over to where I stood. Although my daughter is now five, I can still recall those wonderful images of that day and how proud and excited I felt. I can still see her expression of excitement and great big smile as she stomped her feet.

Allison, Megan's mom

STEP BY STEP

The drive toward independence that started with your baby learning to sit up by himself, then creep, and then crawl is now pushing him toward the finish line of true toddlerhood. The amazing rate of development that you noticed over the past three months will continue as your baby moves toward his first birthday. More than ever, you need to find creative ways to stimulate the neural pathways that are becoming increasingly defined.

It's not hard to become engrossed in play with babies of this age—they are real charmers! But they are also approaching an age (and attention span) where it can be tempting to offer them a video or television show in order to get a little time for yourself. Be alert for any tendencies to do this and try to focus instead on spending time interacting with your baby. (By the way, I'm obviously not opposed to babies of this age viewing appropriate videos! But be sure that you are watching the Baby Prodigy—or other—videos *with* your baby. Take advantage of this rare time when your baby is sitting still to talk about the interesting things that are happening on the screen.) And remember, everything in moderation.

The stimulation you can provide for your baby during these months will enrich him mentally, physically, and emotionally. It is your thoughtful interactions with your baby over the course of any particular day that give him both the tools and the confidence he needs to progress to the next level of growth.

NO STOPPING ME NOW

It's likely that during these months and somewhere around his first birthday, your baby will learn to walk independently. One minute he will be cruising around the room, hanging on to the couch or piano bench, and the next he will be experimenting with letting go and balancing unsteadily on swaying legs. Expect a whole lot of hollering as he looks for his balance and ends up on his behind. And then, probably when you least expect it, you will be privileged to see his excited reaction as he masters his first steps on his own. Once he realizes he can walk, he will want to attempt it again and again. Remember that your cheers and applause will motivate him whenever he accomplishes a few wobbly steps. But if he seems reluctant to repeat this amazing feat, don't push. He will be walking and running before you know it. Too soon. Trust me.

Your baby will also begin to add single recognizable words to her vocabulary during this time, and will hold forth at length—and often at considerable volume—in her own language of vowels and consonants that imitate the tones and rhythms of adult speech. It's likely, too, that one of the first words your baby will utter will be the all-powerful "NO." Even if your baby doesn't master verbal naysaying, you can expect that she will at least learn to shake her head in an emphatic no. Experts refer to this pattern of behavior as "negativism," and you can expect to see it increase in intensity over the next year or so. It's your baby's way of asserting some independence and expressing an opinion. Does she really mean it each time she shakes her head or says no? Probably not, but new words and new head movements are acquired skills—and she needs to practice them, whether it's appropriate or not. You'll quickly learn to discern when a no really means yes.

Your baby will discover new ways to play with his existing toys—whether it's building a stack from the blocks that he used to pass from hand to hand or gnaw on, or initiating a game of "catch" by purposely rolling his ball across the floor to you. On more than one occasion, I peeked around a corner, concerned because my daughter was being so quiet, only to find her immersed in some game of her own invention. As his fine motor dexterity increases, your baby will become more interested in toys and other objects with moving parts. By the end of the twelfth month, he will be trying to understand *how* things work as his concept of causality is strengthening. It's important to spend time explaining things to your baby, even if he doesn't seem to take it all in immediately, as he is truly becoming interested in figuring out what makes things tick.

Your baby will also blossom as a social butterfly during these months—as long as she is secure in the knowledge that you are nearby. If you try to leave her, however, you will quickly be made aware of her growing separation anxiety, which peaks around one year.

By the end of the twelfth month, most babies have mastered the ability to pick up even the tiniest of objects in a precise grip and usually enjoy feeding themselves a wide variety of foods. Your baby may even be experimenting with drinking from a sippy cup or even a regular, baby-sized mug.

Did You Know?: Let Your Baby Be the Boss

Now, before you panic and think I'm encouraging you to raise a pint-sized monarch who insists you bow to her every whim, I want to be clear that I am talking about letting the child take the lead *during designated playtimes only*. In fact, during these next few months, when negativism is first rearing its stubborn little head, you need to be conscious of beginning to set limits and impose discipline in the context of everyday behavior.

However, when you are down on the floor, engrossed with your baby in an interactive game, let her call the shots. You will be helping her to become assertive and to learn to behave in a way motivated by her own desires or emotions. According to experts, connecting emotions to behavior and thought is key in developing creative, critical thinking.

This is a wonderful time for you and your baby to truly enjoy each other's company. The games you have been playing in previous months will become more interactive as the connections in your baby's brain that have been stimulated over and over again grow ever more sophisticated and interconnected.

SLEEPING AND WAKING

During these months your baby's sleeping patterns probably won't differ much from those displayed in the past three months. If your baby still takes a morning and an af-

Your Baby's View: Separation Anxiety

Understanding why your baby becomes anxious when you leave is as simple as putting yourself in her shoes.

Think of all the times during the day (and maybe even at night) when you check in on your baby. Perhaps you are in the kitchen, making a quick list of groceries needed so you can run out and shop. You realize that your baby, who has been crawling around the kitchen, has moved into the dining room. When you stick your head out of the kitchen, your baby catches your eye, gives you a big smile, and returns to her task of putting blocks into a bag. You smile back and return to what you were doing. When you finish, you come out of the kitchen and join her in the dining room. During the day, you and your baby check in with each other dozens of times. Sometimes she crawls after you to see where you're going; sometimes you follow her. You just expect to be able to keep an eye on each other.

Now suppose that your baby is sitting in her favorite spot, filling her bag with blocks. When you check in with her, she smiles but begins dragging her bag across the room. You wonder where she's heading, but seeing your concerned expression, she sits back down and smiles, just like always. Reassured, you return to what you were doing. When you

ternoon nap, he may drop the morning nap around this time. Some babies, however, just love their naps and will happily continue to take two a day. If you find that your baby is having difficulty sleeping at night or is staying up too late at bedtime, you may want to help him to power check for her again, she's gone. Disappeared without a word. You look through the house. No sign of her. You don't know where she is, or if she's coming back. Depending on your personality, your reaction might range from irritation that she didn't check in before she went to another room or sheer panic that she's lost forever. From that moment on, a pattern is established. If she's packing up her blocks, you worry she's planning to leave.

It's not that much of a leap to understand, then, how your baby feels when you leave without letting her know. Your baby will quickly detect the pattern that precedes your leaving her. Usually it's pretty obvious: a babysitter shows up. But even if she's home with your partner, she may notice you picking up your keys or putting on your coat. Even though your leaving may be met with heartbroken sobs and a pitiful clutching at your clothing, it's important that you do not sneak out on your baby. You need to let her know you are going out. Reassure her that she is with someone who cares for her and that you will return. Use the same phrase each time you leave. I always told my daughter, "Mommy is going out now but will come back soon, because Mommy *always* comes back."

After a while, the pattern of your leaving and returning will become acceptable to your baby, and a quick trip to the store will no longer be preceded by a storm of tears and protest.

through his morning without a nap and consolidate his sleep into a bigger block during the night.

Your baby may also have trouble falling asleep on his own, wake during the night, or refuse to settle after awakening in the night. This type of interruption in your baby's

Bye-Bye, Bedtime Bottle

If the end of the twelfth month is approaching, and your baby still depends on sucking on his bottle to fall asleep, it's time to help him to break the habit. Now that he has teeth, it's important to get him in the habit of falling asleep with a clean mouth. Going to sleep with a mouth slick with milk or juice can lead to tooth decay and may even damage your baby's permanent teeth, which are still beneath his gums. Begin to create a new bedtime ritual of tooth washing with a baby toothbrush or washcloth (no toothpaste is necessary, but if you feel compelled, use just the tiniest amount of baby toothpaste) and of mouth rinsing (from a cup! a big-boy cup!). Steel yourself for a few days of pathetic whimpers or crib-shaking rages, depending on your baby's personality, as he gets used to the new routine.

sleep pattern is not unusual and is most likely the result of the growing intensity of any separation anxiety your baby may have. During the day, your baby can crawl around after you, keeping you in view whenever he becomes anxious. However, at night, he is completely alone and confined in his crib, and this may feel more traumatic than daytime separations.

If this is happening with your baby, and leaving him to "cry it out" isn't an option for you, you can go into your baby's room at his first cry and stand by his crib. Rub his back soothingly, but don't engage in conversation. Leave while he is drowsy, but before he falls asleep, so he doesn't become dependent on your presence to drift off.

A bonus by-product of your baby's newfound abilities in sitting, standing, and being able to move toward objects she desires is the increased possibility that she will be able to occupy herself if she wakes with the dawning light and decides she is up for the morning. Leave a few favorite toys or books in her crib at night, and you may just be rewarded with thirty extra minutes of precious shut-eye in the mornings.

STIMULATING YOUR BABY

Your baby's curiosity and appetite for knowledge is amazing to watch. She will become curious about how things work—studying the wheels on a favorite pull-toy or inserting various items into the VCR. She will also watch you closely, mimicking your everyday activities, from talking on the telephone to sweeping the kitchen floor. She will eagerly reach for tidbits of food from your plate, and attempt to insert herself into her older sibling's activities.

As your baby discovers his inner scientist, conducting field studies in every subject from physics (dropping bits of food from his high chair), to anthropology (becoming fascinated with the idea of coloring or writing), to zoology (the relentless pursuit of the family cat), your role becomes that of his ever-helpful research assistant. Provide him with plenty of opportunities to explore things that interest him. Be sure to tell him the names of objects when talking to him, and offer simple explanations for how things work. Try to relate new concepts to ones he is familiar with: "I see you are playing with your red car. The car rolls on the wheels." Show him the wheels as you spin them. "Wheels turn 'round and 'round to make things go. Just like in 'The Wheels on the Bus.' " Then launch into the song.

Of course, the role of a scientific explorer is not without its dangers and pitfalls. Turn back to the previous chapter and review the babyproofing tips (see pp. 122–124). Remember that once your child is standing and walking, a whole new, three-dimensional world of accidents awaits. In the box that follows, I've added a few other tips to make your house safer for a baby who is spending more and more time standing and cruising.

BABY STEPS

From the beginning of the tenth month to the end of your baby's first year, she will attempt to first master and then refine a wide range of activities that expand her areas of independence. From cruising to walking, from eating baby cereal to dinner with the family, from calling the guy at the video store "Dada" to learning to call for "Dada" at five-thirty in the morning when she wants to get out of her crib (and if your baby doesn't know to call for Daddy in those predawn hours, I suggest you teach her how!), your baby is becoming more capable of expressing her opinions and her desires.

By the end of the tenth month, your child should have achieved the milestones listed below. If you are concerned about your child's rate of development, consult your pediatrician. Your baby should be able to:

Safety Watch: Childproofing for Walking Babies

Once your child is up and on her feet, there is so much to discover: shelves full of knickknacks, the tablecloth (and everything on top of it) that covers the dining room table, the kitchen stove ... Every room in the house has many new surfaces to explore. To help keep your baby safe from common hazards, here are some safety tips:

- When cooking, turn all pot handles inward; use back burners only, whenever possible.

- Stove knobs that are within the baby's reach should be babyproofed. This is particularly important on a gas range, where turning the knob slightly may release gas without igniting the burners.

- Never take pills in front of your baby; children mimic what they see. Also, never refer to medicine, vitamins, or over-the-counter medications as "candy."

- Keep dangerous or sharp items away from the edges of tables and countertops, where baby might reach up and grab them.

- Keep trash containers out of baby's reach.

- Move coatracks or tall floor lamps behind large pieces of furniture or otherwise out of the way; your baby can easily tip these over onto herself.

- Remove plastic dry cleaner bags before bringing dry cleaning into the house. This plastic is easy to tear apart and choke on.

Safety Watch: CPR

Don't forget to take a refresher CPR class before the end of your baby's first year. The techniques used for children one year and older can differ slightly from those used for infants.

* pull to a stand from sitting
* stand while holding on to something
* play peekaboo
* move from lying on her stomach to a sitting position
* use a pincer grasp effectively
* cruise (using furniture to balance when walking)
* understand (but not always obey) a simple command, like "No!"
* stand alone without holding on for balance
* balance in a squat while playing
* organize a one-step motor sequence, such as pushing, throwing, or "catching" a ball
* say "Mama" or "Dada" discriminately
* drink from a cup

Sometime between the beginning of the eleventh month and the end of the twelfth month, your baby should be able to perform all of the skills listed above, as well as:

* walk well
* play patty-cake or clap hands

Dookie Says

" 'No, no, no!' That's all I hear. I want to pull the kitty to me; that's why she's got that long tail, right? But as soon as I grab on, Daddy says, 'No, no!' So I crawl over to the window. It should be easy to stand up if I balance using these long curtains. I'm nearly standing, when Mommy runs over, saying, 'No, no!' I wonder if those crayons in my sister's bedroom taste good? I guess I'll never know. I almost had one in my mouth when . . . you guessed it: 'No, no!' How come there's so much to do and they won't let me do any of it?"

It's difficult at this age—and it's only going to get more difficult over the next year or so—to prevent yourself from blurting out an urgent "No!" when you see your baby heading for trouble or mischief. But too much nay-saying can frustrate your adventuresome baby (not to mention it teaches the little mimic a word you'll soon wish he'd never learned). Instead of issuing an immediate "No," try to redirect your baby with gentle instruction: "Kitty doesn't like it when you tug her tail. Let's pet her instead." Or "It's dangerous to pull on the curtains. Try to stand up near the couch." Even if baby can't yet understand the whole meaning of what you're saying, he'll get the idea with your expression and movements as you gently direct him in another direction. The more positive you can be when defining and enforcing these early limits, the more likely it is your baby will be agreeable to following your rules.

* wave bye-bye
* say single words other than "Mama" and "Dada" with discrimination

BABY TALK

As your baby approaches her first birthday, many of you eager parents are awaiting the utterance of her first "real word." Sure, "Mama" and "Dada" made your heart melt, but when there's clearly so much your baby wants to make known, you can't help but think that once she's able to talk, she'll ease up on the frustrated crying and behaviors that she so often directs right at you. Like the time you finally figured out—after much pointing at the refrigerator and its contents—that she wanted milk. And then realized—when your irritated customer hurled her sippy cup across the room in a rage—that she really wanted the yogurt on the shelf *next to* the milk.

I'm afraid I'm going to have to disappoint you here and tell you that it's highly unlikely your baby will have mastered the niceties of verbal communication by the end of her first year. However, all of your interactions and games during the past few months have stimulated the parts of her brain that govern both receptive and productive speech, and you can continue to improve communications and help your baby become confident that she can make herself understood.

Over these few months, your baby's *receptive* speech capabilities will evolve. You can make a simple request such as "Please bring me the shoes," and your baby can let you know that she has heard you and understands. She will either crawl over and get the shoes or glance at the shoes, acknowledging she has heard the request, and then return to what she was .doing—essentially refusing to do the task (see negativism, above).

The more you use gestures and show emotion when you are speaking to your baby, the more receptive she will be to what you are saying. This works equally well whether you are expressing encouragement or enthusiasm or trying to discourage a behavior that is dangerous or unwanted. So, remember, when you are praising your baby—"What a good job of standing up!"—you should also offer her a bright smile and perhaps even a round of applause. By the same token, a frown or a stern expression should accompany a warning: "Don't touch! The radiator is *hot!*" Pay close attention to your baby's reaction. Depending on how attuned she is to your nonverbal communications, you must be prepared to modulate your behavior accordingly.

Your baby's *productive speech*—using her communication skills to make herself understood—is improving as well. She will use facial expressions and gestures, along with babbled sounds, to express herself. Her babbling—or "jargoning," as it is called by some experts—has the inflections and rhythms of speech. Sometimes a few words are even recognizable: "baybeee" or "mama" or "no."

Your baby *wants* to learn speech, and you can help him by repeating the correct word when you hear him make an effort. If he points to his bottle and says "baba," you can respond, "That's right. It's a bottle." Make sure you give positive, not negative reinforcement. You don't want to dampen his enthusiasm by saying "Not baba; say 'bottle.'"

At this stage of language development, remember, it's the thought that counts.

Help your baby develop language skills by remembering these few key concepts:

* **Be an attentive listener.** Pay attention to what your baby is trying to tell you. Respond positively when he makes an effort to get your attention.

* **Label everything.** Tell your baby the name of things, places, colors, and people.

* **Welcome discussion.** Give your baby a chance to respond, either verbally or nonverbally.

GAMES

Opposites Attract

It has probably become obvious to you by this point that babies learn in patterned ways. Introducing *concepts* through play is an excellent way to help your baby begin to make distinctions. Use your imagination and see how many more ways you can illustrate some of the following concepts:

* **In and out.** Put toys in a box, take them out again.

* **Up and down.** Using a Mylar balloon on a string, let it float "up," pull it back "down."

* **Empty and full.** Fill up a cup with water, and then pour it out (particularly good in the tub).

✳ **Happy and sad.** Stand in front of a mirror with your baby. Exaggerate your facial expression. Your baby may begin to mimic you.

✳ **Opposites.** Be creative and make up your own games for this concept.

Easy as One, Two, Three

It's not too early to begin introducing numerical concepts. Count the steps up to the second floor of your house. Count the Cheerios on your baby's high-chair tray. Count the steps down the hall. While he probably won't start doing algebra until grade school, you are laying the groundwork that will help your baby begin to understand the concept of one versus many.

Repeat after Me

Walk around the house with your baby, taking an inventory. Point to a book on the bookshelf and say, "Book." Take a cookbook off the kitchen counter and repeat, "Book." Go into your baby's room and pick up a favorite story and say, "Book." Now go into your room and take the paperback from your nightstand. Hold it up and look puzzled. "What is this?" Give your baby a chance to answer. He might say anything from "bhphftth" to "buh" to "boo" to "gah." No matter the answer, smile, nod, and exclaim with delight *"Yes! Book!"* Celebrate your mutual brilliance and repeat. You can play this game endlessly with all the objects in your house.

Bookshelf

Reading to your baby continues to be important, and over the next few months you may be rewarded with the adorable sight of your baby, sitting quietly in his room, "reading" to himself. Of course he's not actually reading the words, but he's learning valuable lessons like how to turn a page and to recognize the juxtaposition of words and pictures on a page. Because your baby is more mobile and is very intent on exploration, it's good to have your baby's favorite books within easy reach. If you have special editions or particular picture books you want to save, keep them out of reach and bring them out at times when you sit and read together. Your baby will be very interested in books with flaps or pop-up elements, but be warned: These types of books rarely stay intact.

Here are some of my choices for the bookshelf during these months:

- *"More More More," Said the Baby: Three Love Stories* by Vera B. Williams
- *Ten, Nine, Eight* by Molly Bang
- *Where Is Maisy?* by Lucy Cousins
- *Find the Teddy* (and others in this series) by Stephen Cartwright
- *Old Mother Hubbard* by Colin Hawkins and Jacqui Hawkins
- *Peek-a-Boo, You* by Roberta Grobel Intrater

THE LITTLE THINGS: FINE MOTOR SKILLS

With sitting up mastered and her hands free to pick up and explore objects at will, your baby will constantly be looking for new opportunities to examine different items. You will notice that your baby is becoming more precise in her movements. She may attempt to stack one block on top of another, or look for ways to hold a third toy, when she already has one in each hand. Continue to offer her chances to explore textures and shapes, but allow her independence in choosing playthings. Filling a plastic laundry basket with an assortment of favorite toys and household items like plastic spatulas or wooden cooking spoons or plastic containers of various sizes allows your now-mobile baby to access playthings on her own. The idea of taking things out and putting them in is very attractive to babies at this age, and she will enjoy emptying the basket and then returning all the items to the basket over and over again.

Your daily domestic routines will also be of great interest to your baby. Try to involve him by allowing him to mimic your actions. If you are doing laundry, give him an empty basket and a few items of clothing to "sort." When you are cooking, offer him a few pots and pans and a wooden spoon and let him "stir" and bang out rhythms to his heart's content. Grocery shopping can be the highlight of your baby's day, especially if you let him help drop the items into the cart.

Most babies are very interested in watching you write or draw, and your baby may enjoy scribbling with large, easy-to-hold crayons. If your baby is one who is not too fastidious, he may also enjoy finger painting.

Outdoors, you can let her help with yard work, keeping a careful eye on her as she pulls up blades of grass or crumbles dirt from the garden between her fingers. Show her how to pick up tree leaves and release them into the breeze.

Simple musical instruments, like small xylophones, tambourines, or drums, give your baby the opportunity to coordinate movement to create pleasing sounds. Toys that require the pushing of buttons or the twisting of knobs will let your baby practice her fine motor skills. You may have to spend some time demonstrating how a particular activity works, but before long, your baby will develop the hand-eye coordination and concentration necessary to master these types of toys.

If your baby has been learning sign language (see chapter 5), you may be amazed at the sudden surge in his vocabulary as he begins to master more complicated hand movements.

An Important Note of Caution: I see nothing wrong with letting your baby play with common household items, but you must be *very careful* to ensure his safety. Be sure that lids on containers are tightly sealed if small objects are inside, or use empty plastic medicine bottles with child-proof caps. Make sure that containers are clean and free of paper labels that might be gummed off. Avoid using containers or items that held or contain toxic paints or other substances, and be sure nothing has sharp edges. Unless you are completely sure you're offering your baby a totally child-safe toy, do not let your baby out of your sight or reach! Instead, join your baby in his exploration of these fascinating household items.

GAMES

Jam Session

Hand over a couple of pots or some larger plastic containers and a wooden spoon and cover your ears! During these months, your baby's learning is still based in repetition and the discovery of patterns, so don't expect any Charlie Watts–style flourishes yet.

"Handy" Little Entertainments

Hand motion games, like "Itsy-Bitsy Spider" and "Wheels on the Bus," that you have been playing all along with your baby will become even more popular during these few months. Your baby will be likely to join in when you begin a game of patty-cake, clapping along and patting her hands together.

Another favorite to introduce now is "Where is Thumbkin?" Show your baby at first, and then help her to manipulate her fingers through the motions. It will be a while before she can raise each finger independently.

Hold your hands up in two fists and sing (to the tune of "Frère Jacques") *Where is Thumbkin?* (wiggle one thumb). *Where is Thumbkin?* (wiggle the other thumb). *Here I am. Here I am* (make your thumbs "bow" to each other). *How are you today, sir? Very well I say, sir. Run away* (hide one hand behind your back). *Run away* (hide the other hand behind your back). Bring both hands out and

Toy Chest

As your baby heads toward her first birthday, she is learning mostly by mimicking. As she watches you go about your daily routines, she may demand to try to hold the broom or crawl off with the dustpan, or insist on unfolding the clothes that are neatly stacked in the laundry basket. For the next few months, she will happily play with whatever she sees you "playing" with. With her interested in mobility and intent on standing, cruising, and walking, your whole house has potential as a play structure, and the most common items become objects of desire. Whether you let your baby "help out" by giving her full-sized objects or you hit the toy stores in search of mini items, most babies will enjoy playing with the following:

- vacuum cleaners they can push around (be aware, however, that your baby may be sensitive to, or even afraid of, the sound of the vacuum)

start again with "Where is Pointer?" Repeat for all five fingers.

The Life of the Party

You're never too young—or old—for a rousing game of pin the tail on the donkey. Make sure to hang the picture of the donkey low enough that your crawling baby can reach it. Use double-sided tape to make it easy for her to stick the tail on. Be creative and invent new games: pin the

- unbreakable plates, cups, and other containers
- wooden spoons for stirring
- pots and pans
- toy telephones
- rag dolls
- miniature plastic foods
- household items with buttons, like TV remotes or calculators (if you give your baby a remote or any battery-operated object, remember to remove the batteries, as they can become dangerous if chewed or broken by baby's inquisitive fingers)
- key rings with old keys
- a wallet filled with expired membership cards or even pieces of colored cardboard (No coins, ever!)

blanket on the donkey's back, or pin the flower on the donkey's ear. Besides encouraging manual dexterity, this is a great hand-eye coordination exercise, as your child tries to stick the tails (ears, blankets, flowers, etc.) on the correct part of the picture.

Feeding the Birds

Make some feathered friends when you head out to the park, duck pond, or backyard. Show your child how to crumble up crackers or stale bread. Let your child take the crackers out of the box or the bread out of the bag and work at throwing small pieces.

Just Another Day at the Office

Give your child an old computer keyboard and let her bang out a few memos. Keep a close eye on her so she doesn't pull any caps off the keys or otherwise work any small parts loose. While she's typing, talk about some of the letters she is pressing.

HOW IT ALL FITS: SPATIAL DEVELOPMENT

Due to all the motor development and movement that he is mastering over these next few months, your baby is now working on spatial development in new dimensions. He has to learn that to crawl under a table, he will need to duck his head. He will spend time figuring out just how far he has to go to lower himself from a stand to the floor. And once he begins to walk . . . well, then there's those tricky questions of just how close he is to a sharp edge or solid object as he starts to lose his balance. No question about it: This is a stressful time, full of bumps, bruises, and, quite likely, unexpected trips to the pediatrician or emergency room. One mother I know joked that her son would have benefited from an emergency room frequent-flier-type program during the months when he was learning to walk. The best advice I can offer is to stay calm and encouraging as your intrepid athlete attempts seemingly impossible feats of balance and speed. And don't forget to have a ready supply of ice, antibacterial ointment, and Band-Aids!

When your baby isn't scooting, crawling, standing, or

walking (or falling), she is likely to be exploring hand-eye coordination. She will be interested in putting things in and taking them out. She will put lids on pots, books in the VCR slot, and toys in the toilet (unless you're careful!). Although she may not be able to sort different shapes, she will clearly grasp the purpose of shape-sorter toys and, with your guidance, may enjoy fitting the shapes into their various holes.

Keep playing music and musical games with your baby. Researchers believe that music can help prime the neural pathways that play a role in spatial reasoning. Classical music in particular seems to enhance certain kinds of thinking. Studies have shown that after listening to classical music, adults are able to perform certain spatial tasks—like putting together a jigsaw puzzle—more quickly. Researchers think the complexity of the structure of classical music is what stimulates the brain to solve spatial problems more easily. So be certain to keep music a big part of your baby's life. The benefits can be both immediate and long-lasting.

GAMES

Soccer Star

Support your baby under his arms and let him kick a light-weight ball or Mylar balloon. Switch around to let him be goalie and gently roll the ball or balloon toward him as he sits on the floor. He will reach toward it to catch or stop it before it rolls past him.

Puzzle Solver

Your baby may be ready to try placing large wood puzzle pieces in their correct spots. Picture puzzles that have the same picture on the board (so when you lift the puzzle piece you can see the same picture) give your baby a visual cue as to where each piece belongs. At first you will have to help him replace each piece of the puzzle, but before long, your baby will be able to try a few variations in order to get the piece to fit.

Kitchen Chemistry

Set your baby up with pots with lids, plastic containers with lids, measuring spoons that are attached on a ring, and plastic mixing bowls that nest one inside the other. Bring out the towels and dare to fill a few of the pots with a small amount of water. Offer measuring cups that can be used to scoop and dump. Your baby and your kitchen floor may get a little wet, but I can guarantee that your budding chef will have a great time.

GET UP AND GO: GROSS MOTOR SKILLS

At some point over the last few months, you probably paused midway up a flight of stairs or jumped on a bus, having run half a block to catch it, gazed down at the chunky baby in your arms, waited to catch your breath, and then sighed, "I can't wait until you can walk."

All I can say is "Be careful what you wish for!"

Whether your baby walks well before a year or several

months after his first birthday, his first steps herald an important stage of development. Much like the evolution of man to an upright posture, your baby's ability to get up off the floor where he has spent most of the past year opens new horizons that are unbelievably exciting.

And although it seems like those first steps happen overnight, walking does not happen all of a sudden. For the past few months your baby has been practicing and trying out the components of walking. But it's a process of trial and error. Continuing to offer your baby positive stimulation during this time will allow him to develop confidence in the sequence of walking and allow him to happily master this ultimate achievement of sensory and motor abilities.

If your child isn't walking around the one-year mark, don't worry. Not all babies are in such a hurry to be upright and mobile. If your baby has always been laid-back in temperament and is crawling or scooting to get where he wants to go, try to be patient and think of this as a grace period before you are hurled into the constant motion that is toddlerhood.

Some babies may also begin to show an interest in climbing. Once your baby can pull to a stand, it's a good idea to remove all extra blankets, crib bumpers, and large stuffed toys from the crib. Some particularly adept little gymnasts may even figure out how to get out of the crib by their first birthday. Don't make it any easier for them!

Dottie Says

"Now that I'm walking I can't help but notice all of Mommy's beautiful shoes. Whenever I can, I get into her closet and play with them. I can't wait to wear my own shoes. I think I'd like some cowboy boots and some ballet slippers and some high-heeled sparkly pumps and maybe some little strappy sandals and most certainly a pair of tall boots. Yes, now that I can walk, I definitely need a shoe for every occasion."

Now it's just possible that you can't bring yourself to walk past a shoe sale. But if you've been thinking that just because your baby is walking, you can justify your craving for a pair of adorable suede loafers by buying them for her, or if you expect your new walker to share your shoe fetish, well, it's only fair to warn you that you're likely to be disappointed. In fact, the best kind of shoe for a new walker to wear is no shoe at all. Your baby will, in fact, start out using her toes to grip the floor as she practices standing. The more flexibility her feet have, the more she can count on them to help her find her balance. As long as her feet are warm and she is on a safe, clean surface, your baby is best off barefoot. If she will be outdoors, or needs shoes for a special occasion (I admit it, I couldn't resist those tiny patent leather Mary Janes with bows), then try to find shoes that have the following features:

- flexible soles that bend when your baby takes a step
- leather, canvas, or cloth uppers that can breathe and have give
- nonskid bottoms
- padded back and side edges
- plenty of room
- a cut that doesn't inhibit ankle movement

Games Siblings Play

Until your baby is steady on his feet and walking proficiently, this can be a tricky time to keep sibling play civilized. You'll need to stay close by to ensure that your older child doesn't interfere with your baby's attempts to balance. Watch out for roughhousing or any way of "helping" the baby to walk that is really only a thinly veiled excuse for dragging him across the room. For the next few months, encourage floor games that let your baby interact with his big brother or sister in a more equal way. Here are a couple of suggestions for games that are fun for both the large and small participants:

- **Robo-baby.** Purchase a remote-controlled toy, like a race car. Allow your older child to operate the remote and encourage your baby to crawl after the toy. This game does require your supervision, especially as you teach your baby that the point is to chase the toy, not catch it and claim it. And teach your older child that the point is not to run over his younger sibling with the toy!

- **Upstairs, downstairs.** You can play this game only if you have baby gates at the top and bottom of your staircase (which you should!) and are willing to supervise the entire time, but it does teach your baby a valuable skill she eventually needs to master. Have your older child crawl up the stairs on his hands and knees to demonstrate to your baby how to climb up. Once she has the hang of going up, challenge your older child to demonstrate safe ways to come back down the stairs, like bumping down on his bottom, or turning around and crawling back down feetfirst. It won't be long before your baby is proficient at going up and down the staircase in a "safe" manner.

> • **Bath-time brouhaha.** It's likely that your baby already loves
> bath time. Make it twice as fun by letting your older child
> join the baby in the tub. Give them plastic cups for pour-
> ing, toys for floating, or blowing bubbles. Be prepared for a
> wet bathroom floor, as splashing is inevitable!

GAMES

A Stroll(er) around the Park

Instead of keeping your baby buckled into her stroller the
entire time you are out, look for a grassy spot and let her experiment with standing and walking, using her stroller for
support. Remember that if she is pushing her stroller out in
front of her, she can't see where she's going. Nor does she
know how to control her forward momentum. So keep
your hand on the handle of the stroller to keep it all under
control.

For Budding Gymnasts

You may be able to find a parents' group or other playgroup
that has climbing and crawling equipment suitable for
your baby. When our daughter was this age, I purchased a
plastic baby climber with a short slide. Although this was
an outdoor toy, I moved it right into the playroom, and it
kept us busy all winter long. My daughter loved crawling
through the holes, hiding underneath, and wriggling her
way onto the platform and down the slide. Don't let bad
weather put a damper on your baby's physical activity.

Ride 'Em, Cowboy

Toward the end of your baby's first year, he may become interested in sitting on sturdy riding toys that can scoot, roll, or rock. He will need your help at first, both for balance in getting on and off the toys and in making them move. Make sure the toys have rounded edges and are quite low to the ground (easy for him to swing a little leg over and not so tall that a little tumble becomes a big deal), and never let your baby use them near stairs or other inclines. Don't be surprised if your baby isn't ready to coordinate all the steps needed to properly operate a ride-on toy. For the next few months he may just enjoy crawling on and over it or even just sitting on that cute stuffed rocking horse you got him.

Bubble-Wrap Hoedown

Tape a piece of bubble wrap (with the big bubbles) to the floor and have a rootin', tootin', stompin' good time.

Beanbag Basketball

Practice tossing an easy-to-grab beanbag into a trash can. Start out with a trash can that's low to the ground, or even a laundry basket, and work your way up to a taller, narrower "hoop." Show your child how he can throw underhand, toss overhand, or slam dunk!

chapter seven

The Great Communicator: Thirteen through Eighteen Months

Sometimes the first word doesn't come quickly enough for us parents. We are always coaxing and waiting, and then, when we least expect it, it comes out of the blue. My daughter Lara was always very quiet. We were always waiting for that one word we could understand besides "Mama" and "Dada." One Saturday afternoon we were in the car. I was driving, Barbara was in the passenger seat, and Lara was sitting quietly in her car seat in back. All of a sudden someone screamed, "CARRRR-RRRRRRRR!!!!" The word was perfectly clear and shouted with urgency. My car swerved wildly as I frantically looked from side to side, shouting, "WHERE? WHERE'S THE CAR?" Once I had calmed down, I shot Barbara a dirty look; she knows it makes me crazy when she comments on my driving. But she didn't seem to be taking me too seriously; in fact, she was laughing pretty hard.

"It wasn't me, it was Lara!" she said. And I started to laugh, too. In the midst of our laughter, Lara began to holler, "CAR, CAR, CAR!" From that day forward, it was her favorite word. It certainly got everyone's attention.

Richard, Samantha and Lara's dad

BYE-BYE, BABY

I'll admit it: I wanted to be able to think of my active, vocal one-year-old as a sweet, compliant baby—unfortunately, she seemed to have other ideas! From voicing strong opinions about what she ate, to what she wore, to where she went, my precious little baby had turned into a strong-willed individual who—if I wasn't willing to get her what she wanted—would simply stroll across the room, climb the bookshelf, and get it herself! If you're reading this and nodding your head knowingly—well, welcome to toddlerhood!

This is an amazing period of development in your child's life. Every minute of every day is an opportunity for learning and exploring, and your child is eager to experience it all for himself. Sometimes all this stimulation can be overwhelming, though, and at those times your "baby" returns, needing cuddles, reassurance, and support.

As your baby moves into being a toddler, the most important advice I can offer to you is "Don't rush it!" It is just as important now that you be attuned to your child's moods and needs as it was when he was a helpless infant. Obviously, the way you relate to your child has evolved into a more interactive relationship. Now you'll talk together, walk together, and play together—learning to understand and respect each other's opinions and ideas. The thing that hasn't changed is the importance of your role in stimulating your toddler as his brain continues to develop in increasingly sophisticated ways.

IN LEAPS AND BOUNDS

This period, from the beginning of the thirteenth month through the end of the eighteenth month, represents a particularly intense learning period for a toddler. He has a greater command over his motor skills as he learns to walk, run, or climb to get what he wants. Your toddler is driven to practice these skills, often to the point of exhaustion and teary breakdown. Bumps and bruises continue to be commonplace over these months, and you may have grown more relaxed about the spectacular tumbles practiced by your early walker.

Your child can operate her arms and hands with ease, reaching out and grasping whatever interests her and exploring it in detail. Games that involve taking out and putting back in are still of great interest to the one- to one-and-a-half-year-old child.

Your toddler may be sleeping somewhat less, leaving more time for exploring. And explore he will. Not because he has a particular purpose in mind, but simply because there are so many things to look at, touch, smell, taste, and listen to. His senses are in a constant state of stimulation.

Everything is new to your little explorer, and it's important that you provide a variety of stimulation for all his senses as he plays and learns.

Over these few months, you may also notice a shift from exploring to experimenting. Your toddler is relying on her memory (short as it is at this point) as a point of reference. She may begin to recognize similarities and differences in objects and start to organize her world by comparing, contrasting, and sorting.

By about fifteen months, toddlers can recognize themselves in a mirror. Along with this increased self-awareness comes an awareness of others. They begin to have an interest in other children and will be willing to play with them. At first this play takes the form of playing alongside a companion, each child involved in separate activities, called "parallel play," and later it evolves into true social interaction.

Your child's increasing language skills, both in understanding and using speech, will also be developing in a sophisticated way as she begins to link words to objects, emotions, and overall context.

SLEEPING AND WAKING

At the start of toddlerhood, your child will begin extending her awake time and cutting back her sleep time. For instance, if she is napping twice a day at one year, by the end of the eighteenth month, she may be ready to give up her morning nap or consolidate her morning and late afternoon nap into one longer, midday snooze.

Did You Know?: Your Toddler's Senses

Interacting with your child in ways that stimulate her senses to promote maximum mental development is just as important now as it was when she was an infant, first learning about the world. Before you read on and see how intensely and instinctively your toddler uses her senses, I want you to take a moment and look back to chapter 2. From birth, your baby has relied on her senses to navigate an unknown world, and throughout this book, I've offered you age-appropriate ways to stimulate your child's senses. Now, after a year, it's amazing to consider the developments that have taken place since those early weeks.

Sight

- Your toddler has 20/20 vision, but his visual attention is still untrained. Anything in his field of vision is equally attention-worthy. He spends all day being bombarded with images. While his eyesight is keen, he still needs help with focus.

- The concept of perspective is forming in your toddler's mind. She can recognize herself (or you) when looking in a mirror.

- Familiar objects are easily recognizable, even when viewed from peculiar angles. Your toddler is very interested in objects that are revealed in ways that change their everyday appearance, such as toys viewed through a sheer curtain, or his own elongated shadow.

Hearing

- Your toddler's ears are assaulted with sounds, and it can be difficult for him to focus on a single auditory stimulus.

It's amazing to think that the baby who would startle when you turned on the vacuum cleaner now barely acknowledges you when you call his name from two feet away!

- Most toddlers like listening to, and making, music. The music you used to stimulate or soothe your child when she was an infant will be just as effective now that she is a toddler.

- Your child can probably identify some common sounds and react appropriately. For instance, pointing at the door when the doorbell rings. Or saying "Dada?" expectantly when she hears a car in the driveway.

Smell

- Unlike the sensitive baby nose that could recognize her mother's breast milk, your toddler's sense of smell is somewhat less discerning. You need to take care, since your young scientist is just as interested in smelling cleaning fluid or nail polish remover as he is in stopping to smell the roses.

Taste

- The baby that was so adventurous in tasting new bits of finger foods may have morphed into a toddler with a limited palate. Offer but don't force new foods and continue to entice your toddler with foods of varying textures, colors, and shapes. Just as infants may show a preference for sweets, your toddler may have discovered the joys of sugar. No matter how much he'd prefer candy to veggies, hold firm and limit sweet treats.

Touch

- While your infant may have loved being touched, your toddler loves to do the touching. Exploring through tactile
  sensation is incredibly important. Unfortunately, this type
  of exploration frequently includes tearing pages out of
  magazines, pulling hairs out of the cat, or reprogramming
  the VCR. Try to create a childproofed environment in your
  home where touching is never off limits and there is an assortment of safe objects that will let your child explore
  concepts such as soft, smooth, scratchy, or nubby.

Although your active toddler needs between ten and
twelve hours of sleep each night, his newfound physical
talents may allow him to discover how to climb in and out
of his crib, making middle-of-the-night or super-early-in-
the-morning waking a bit harder to deal with. (Because
even though they know how to climb *in* as well as *out,* my
girls only ever seemed to want to practice the *out* part!)
Unfortunately, if your child is an accomplished crib es-
caper, there's little you can do about it. Some children's
specialty stores sell tents that you can put over the top of a
crib. These lightweight fabric screens may help to discourage untimely escapes.

There are a few other challenges that center around
sleep that you may encounter over these months: difficulty
with transitions from napping to awake, and the common
toddler problem of becoming overtired.

Transitioning from being asleep to awake and vice
versa can be hard even for adults, so it's reasonable to ex-

pect it to be a challenge for your little one. The key is to gently ease them in and out, just as you would want to be gradually awakened and allowed to fall asleep. If you need to wake your toddler from a long nap (either because of your schedule or because if she keeps sleeping she'll be up all night!), be sure to allow for at least a half hour of cuddling and quiet attention to help her transition from being snug in her cozy bed to loose and on the move.

It's difficult to prevent these little busybodies from becoming overtired, which can lead to trouble sleeping. Your toddler is so busy practicing his new skills that he will often push himself to the point of physical exhaustion. Be alert for a drop in coordination, especially when combined with exciting or tense situations. Your toddler cannot recognize that he is tired and will not stop and rest. You need to rescue him—or risk a total meltdown. Over these next few months, you can try introducing the concept of quiet time—moments when your toddler can rest and recharge without actually taking a nap. Go into your child's room with him and spend quiet time just sitting. You can read, or talk, or listen to a music or story tape. If you're lucky, your toddler may adapt to this idea, and you'll be able to convince him to spend this quiet time in his room alone.

STIMULATING YOUR TODDLER

The key word for stimulating your toddler over the next few months and into the second year is "encouragement." Toddlers learn through exploration and opportunity, so provide her with a safe space in which she can move and

Toddler R&R

What's the key to being a well-rested and refreshed parent? Having a well-rested and refreshed toddler! The following tips are as useful for stressed-out adults as they are for overtired tots:

- Wake up at the same time each day. Yes, even on weekends.

- Go to bed at the same time each night. Okay, grown-ups, you can have a little more leeway on this one—but only by an hour or so.

- Don't keep going until you're frantic. If a task is getting too frustrating, take a break.

- Recharge when your batteries are lowest. If you—or your toddler—have a midafternoon lull and just can't keep your eyes open, don't reach for caffeine or plop your child down in front of a stimulating video. Instead give in to the call of your biorhythms and take a brief but refreshing nap.

explore. She will delight in crawling under, climbing over, and bouncing around.

Encourage your child's newly discovered independence by providing him with accessible baskets of toys, books, and other playthings. Let him enjoy his new ability to choose what he would like to examine and practice his freedom to pick something out of the basket and drop it to the floor with a satisfying *thump*. Your toddler's attention span is improving, and he can concentrate on a single toy for a brief period of time. But while he will take the time

A Few Words about Discipline

There are entire books devoted to techniques for instilling a sense of discipline in toddlers. And having survived two toddlers of my own, I can see why it's needed. If you are looking for a game plan for taming a particularly difficult toddler, check the appendix at the back of this book for some ideas on where to start. In the meantime, here are a few words to bear in mind when your toddler's natural curiosity is about to get the best of both of you:

- **Restrain.** Yourself, that is. Don't immediately resort to yelling, "No, no!" or "Don't!" or "Stop!" expecting your child to stop in the middle of what he is doing. A toddler loves a challenge and won't necessarily back off from further confrontation. Always be prepared to back up your words with action. Don't allow yourself to become angry, categorize your child as "bad," or jump on every little infraction. Choose your battles when setting limits and be consistent.

- **Refrain.** As in the chorus of a song. Toddlers have limited memories, so you can't expect them to remember all the rules all the time. Be prepared to repeat the same message over and over again. Again, consistency is the key to helping toddlers understand what is and isn't appropriate.

- **Retrain.** What I really mean here is "redirect," but I couldn't resist the rhyme! When your toddler's headed for trouble, you need to head him off first with another, equally intriguing option. Eventually your child will understand that while it's not okay to bang on the TV screen or windowpanes with his toy hammer, he is allowed to hammer away at pots and pans, or blocks of wood, or even the kitchen floor.

to examine an object or a toy before moving on to the next, he still does not have a long memory, and so you may notice that he will keep coming back to the same toy with equal enthusiasm over and over again. This means there's no need to include every toy in the toy box. A better idea is to rotate a succession of favorite toys, so he always has something "new" to explore.

Encourage and stimulate your toddler's language boom by responding to her questions, babbles, and commands using a grown-up voice and grown-up words. Listen carefully when she talks to you, make eye contact, and respond, even if you're not one hundred percent sure what she's said. When you think you do know what she's saying, repeat her request back to her in other words. For instance you might respond to a request for "mo meee" by saying, "Would you like more milk?" Read to her and label common objects seen in your home, on your walks, and in the grocery store. Sing songs or chant rhymes; the repetition and rhythmic tones will capture your child's attention as it helps her vocabulary grow. Greet your toddler's verbal efforts with enthusiasm and encouragement, and you'll soon have a confident communicator.

TODDLER STEPS

From the beginning of the thirteenth month to the end of the eighteenth, your child will be rapidly developing her mobility, her fine motor skills, and her speech. And it's probably not happening in the same kind of steady linear progression that was so satisfying to chart in her baby book

Toy Chest

The best toys for your toddler are simple things that let him explore his world, begin to understand how things work, establish context, and mimic grown-up routines. Here are some easy-to-find items and toys that I've used with my girls for hours of fun and stimulating learning:

- **Water.** It can be plain, bubbly, iced, colored, cool, warm. Let your child splash, pour, measure, spill, float things, or immerse herself (all under supervision, of course!).

- **Mud, clay, or dough.** Roll, squish, mold, and shape it. You can make your own safe Play-Doh or buy commercial brands, or just go outside and get filthy playing in some good squishy mud.

- **Sand.** Pile it, pour it, make it wet. If you can't get to the beach, fill a box with sand and have a sandbox in your backyard or, on rainy days, your own mini-island in the middle of the kitchen. Keep a toy broom handy for the inevitable sandstorm on the kitchen floor.

during the early months. That's because she's not really a baby anymore—she's a toddler! And toddlers develop in uneven leaps and bounds, perhaps taking a few unsteady steps one day and, a few weeks later, running across the lawn as they chase their favorite ball. Children in this age range can vary widely in their development, so the lists below purposely cover a variety of skills.

Your baby who was walking by her first birthday may

- **Blocks.** Stack them up, knock them down, pound them, line them up. Choose small, easy-to-hold wooden blocks with animal pictures or letters of the alphabet on them and they can be used in whole new ways as your child grows.

- **Sorting toys.** Provide simple wooden shapes that fit easily into large holes. You will still have to help with maneuvering the shapes to fit into the holes, but your child may begin to recognize and match the shapes. You can use foam board and cut out the outlines of simple shapes such as squares, circles, and triangles. Help your child replace the shapes, like you're solving a simple jigsaw puzzle.

- **Cups and other containers.** Fill, empty, or pour from one to another. Your toddler will begin to grasp concepts like full and empty.

- **Light balls, beanbags, or Mylar balloons.** Catch, throw, and kick.

- **Crayons, finger paints, and paper.** Scribbling is an exciting exercise in cause and effect for your toddler.

be running by the time she is fifteen months old. Another child may not run with confidence until he is a year and a half or older. But he may have an extensive vocabulary and be using simple two-word sentences by the time he is sixteen months. Because there is such a wide range of developmental ability at this age, don't make yourself crazy by comparing your child solely against this list, or even against one or two or her friends.

You have spent a year with this little person, and you,

better than anyone else, know if she is developing appropriately, based upon her personality and physical strengths and weaknesses.

Of course, as you know by now from reading the earlier chapters, if you ever have any questions or concerns about your child's rate of development, you should consult your pediatrician.

Somewhere between the beginning of the thirteenth month and the end of the fifteenth month, your child should have achieved many of the milestones listed below. Your toddler should be able to:

* easily pull up to standing
* cruise with confidence
* play patty-cake
* scribble with a crayon
* sort objects into containers
* build a stack of two or more blocks
* walk well
* walk up steps with help
* climb
* run
* use simple sentences ("What that?" or "Give me.")
* understand and (sometimes) follow simple commands

Sometime between the beginning of the sixteenth month and the end of the eighteenth month, your child should be able to perform all of the skills listed above as well as be able to:

Did You Know?:
Development of Premature Babies

If your baby was born prematurely, you may find that he is not reaching the milestones listed in each chapter in this book within the expected age range.

Although you and your pediatrician are no doubt carefully monitoring your baby's development, there are certain delays that are common among premature infants that may especially stand out as they move into toddlerhood. Conditions that are often present in premature children and that gradually resolve over the first two years of life may include:

- abnormal muscle tone
- mild delays in growth
- mild delays in achievements of skill
- behavioral problems that may inhibit attaining milestones

Many parents and pediatricians evaluate a preemie's development according to a scale of "adjusted age." That is, a baby who was born two months premature and who is now fourteen months old would be an adjusted age of twelve months and would be reaching milestones accordingly. By the time a child is two or older, she has generally caught up from any mild or temporary developmental delays.

If your toddler is frustrated by any of the games or activities suggested in this chapter, review earlier chapters for ideas on how to tailor the stimulation you provide to suit his attention and abilities. Remember, helping your child reach his potential is not just about having a smarter baby; it's about having a happier baby as well.

Dottie Says

"Ooh, look what I've found in Daddy's pocket. It's his phone. Wow, I love pushing all these buttons. Oh, cool, it's ringing. Someone's talking! 'Bah, Ma-ma-ma-ma, ah-gook, no! No! Bye.' Gee, that was fun. Now which button did I push again?"

Once your highly imitative toddler becomes enamored of your phone, or PDA, or remote control, you need to be sure that the versions she is allowed to play with are completely disabled. Or take your chance with the consequences.

Here's an unbelievable-but-true baby and phone story: Our one-year-old daughter snagged her dad's cell phone. My husband was in the other room talking to a client on the house phone, and I overheard the whole exchange. First my husband said to his client, "Sure, I'll hold." Then I heard our daughter babbling away, obviously in intent conversation. How cute it was that she was imitating her dad! A few minutes later I heard my husband laughing and exclaiming, "What do you mean, it was a baby on the line?" By now our daughter had abandoned the cell phone and moved on to another activity. And then it dawned on me. I picked up the cell phone and checked the call log, and sure enough, my husband had been put on hold so his client could take a speed-dialed call from our one-year-old daughter!

* drink from a cup
* remove a piece of her clothing
* throw a ball overhand
* use a spoon

* kick a ball forward
* name body parts
* name an object in a picture
* have a vocabulary of up to fifty recognizable words

TODDLER TALK

Beginning to use language appropriately—like excitedly yelling out "CAR!" when she sees one on the highway (okay, so maybe it's not always *appropriate*)—is a hallmark of your toddler's verbal development. From babbling with a conversational tone but few recognizable words, to issuing commands like a mini-Mussolini—"Me go!" "Cookie!" "Juice!"—your toddler is learning how words, concepts, emotions, and actions interact. Like most developing skills over these months, toddlers' verbal talents may vary widely. One mother claims her son never said a word until his eighteenth month, when one morning he calmly told her, "I don't like cereal. I want toast and butter."

Another mother recalls how she wished for earplugs just for a few hours of relief from the nonstop chatter of her fifteen-month-old daughter, whose earliest words included, "What's that?" Worn down by her daughter's relentless quest to have everything in her field of vision labeled—"That's a couch." "That's a crack in the sidewalk." "That's salmon steak."—the beleaguered mom would beg her little darling to "Please, please, let's just be quiet for one minute," as other parents commented on how nice it was to have such a talkative toddler.

Whether you're coaxing your strong, silent type to say

a few words or rapidly feeding the voracious vocabulary of an early talker, you can still provide important stimulation that will help your toddler learn how to truly communicate and understand the importance of language.

In the beginning of this second year and up until the end of the eighteenth month, it is likely that new words will come slowly. But each new word that is learned is practiced with a variety of intonations, as your child learns to communicate emotions and meanings. Consider the following variations of a simple word:

"Dog!" exclaimed in excitement might mean: "I see a dog."

"Dog?" could be asking: "Is the dog coming over to me?"

"Dog!" accompanied by a disappointed shake of the head and exasperated tone might mean: "The dog went the other way."

It is your job to help your budding linguist communicate clearly by mirroring back to her the intent of her comments. For example, when she says "Dog!" while out walking, you can repeat back, "Yes, that's a dog," or "Yes, I see the dog, too."

By around eighteen months, your child will likely experience a huge jump in the number of words she knows, from around 30 to around 200 (or, in some cases, 400 or more). The numbers continue to increase exponentially. By the time your child starts kindergarten, she will have a vocabulary of more than 2,000 words. If your child isn't saying any words by fifteen months (including "Mama" or

"Dada"), didn't babble before his first birthday, or makes only unintelligible sounds (even to you), you may want to discuss his speech development with your pediatrician. Among other possibilities, your child's hearing may be impaired, making imitative speech difficult or impossible.

Books continue to be important learning tools, and reading becomes much more interactive. Your toddler can now identify pictures in the books that interest her, pointing to various objects, and you can use these opportunities to encourage your child to answer simple questions. For instance, when your thirteen-month-old points to a cat, ask her, "What does the cat say?" Your eighteen-month-old might be able to answer a question as complex as "What color is the cat?" Use your imagination when reading and be creative with how you use your toddler's favorite books.

GAMES

Hello, Who's Calling, Please?

One of the most interesting items to toddlers is a phone. The allure of talking on the phone, whether it's your home telephone or a cell phone, is irresistible. Toy stores offer many versions of pretend phones, but I found that my kids were most satisfied by the real thing. An old phone without a cord or a cell phone with the battery removed will quickly become a favorite toy. Hold your own phone as you pretend to call your child and engage her in conversations. This is a great opportunity to model basic good manners, such as saying "Hello, How are you?," and "Good-bye" appropriately.

What Comes Next?

Use your imagination and find lots of times to play this game. I used it most often when getting my children dressed in the morning. Ask your child, "What does [child's name] wear next?" as you look at her clothes. Your child may point to an item of clothing, and you can tell her, "Yes, the diaper comes next," as you put on her diaper. Continue asking the question and naming all her pieces of clothing as you get her dressed for her day. Try this game in reverse at night: "What comes off next?"

Show and Tell

Help your child connect words and actions by offering a play-by-play of your daily activities. "Mommy is making a sandwich for lunch"—go into the kitchen. "We need bread"—show slices of bread. "I cut some tomato with a knife"—show tomato and knife—and so on. You may feel silly carrying on a monologue at first, but as your child's vocabulary increases, start offering places where he can fill in the blanks. For example, if you are going outside, begin by saying, "Mommy is putting on her . . ." and then hold up your shoe and pause, seeing if your child can fill in the blank.

Where Is It? What Is It?

Another naming game that is a particularly good distraction at bath time is to ask your child, "Where is [child's name]'s nose?" At first you will touch your child's nose, or elbow, or fingers, or toes each time after you ask the ques-

Bookshelf

Over the past year, it has probably become apparent what your toddler is most interested in. For some children it's trucks, cars, or emergency vehicles; one of my daughters was crazy about kittens; the other couldn't get enough of farm animals; and I know several toddlers who were fascinated with dinosaurs before they could talk. This is a great time to indulge your child's interests through books. Toddlers are generally so active that reading time may take a backseat to playtime. But if you follow your child's lead and choose books that interest him, you will be able to maintain a ritual of reading together, even with the most active of toddlers. Here are a few of my favorite books for this age:

- *Dig Dig Digging* by Margaret Mayo and Alex Ayliffe
- *Who Said Moo?* by Harriet Ziefert and Simms Taback
- *Sleepy Me* by Marni McGee
- *My First Word Touch and Feel* from Dorling Kindersley
- *Hello, Lulu* by Caroline Uff
- *The Baby's Word Book* by Sam Williams

tion. Before you know it, your child will be touching the correct body part at your prompting. And soon after that, he may begin to be able to answer verbally if you point to his nose and ask, "What is this?"

THE LITTLE THINGS: FINE MOTOR SKILLS

With her hands now completely under her control and with complete confidence in her ability to reach, grasp, hold, and drop items, your toddler is actively engaging in a wide range of activities that help hone her developing fine motor skills. Over these few months, your child will particularly enjoy putting things in and taking them out of containers, imitating the act of drawing or writing by attempting her own scribbling, stacking, sorting, and stringing. It's easy to provide her with opportunities to practice all these skills without investing in expensive toys or activity boards. I found this stage particularly helpful, as it was the perfect opportunity to begin to teach my toddlers how to help with cleanup. No matter how many toys were scattered throughout the house, my daughter was more than willing to follow me around and help me collect toys in the big plastic laundry basket we used as her toy box.

Use the following list of activities to inspire your own creativity in stimulating your busy toddler.

* **Putting in and taking out.** Have an assortment of boxes, containers, and paper bags available to your child, and offer a variety of objects of different weights and sizes.

* **Scribbling.** Tape paper securely to a table or the floor and let your child use extra-thick crayons to experiment with cause and effect as she moves the crayon across the page.

* **Stacking.** Let your child play with wooden or cardboard blocks, toys that stack one inside the other, and plastic containers of varying size.

* **Sorting.** Give your toddler different-colored socks, different shapes of pasta, different kinds of cereal, or other objects of varying size.

All these activities will reinforce the brain wiring that is taking place as your toddler's fine motor coordination develops, so don't think you have to direct your child to any one particular activity. Remember, repetition is key for your toddler in mastering any task. The games below offer some simple activities your toddler will enjoy and that promote manual dexterity.

GAMES

Architect at Work

Use wooden blocks to create simple patterns, such as rows, towers, or pyramids. Encourage your child to imitate your structures and then let him build his own design for you to copy.

Speed Racers

Empty paper towel tubes are just the right size to use as tunnels for small toy cars or balls. (If your child is still putting things in her mouth, supervise her carefully, as items that can fit through a cardboard tube of this size can pose a choking hazard.) Hold the tube steady and let your child drop items into it, then watch as they shoot out the other end.

Grocery Bagger

The next time you grocery shop, put cans and lightweight paper products in the same bag. Put the bag on the floor and let your child help you unpack. You'll be able to get all the other groceries put away without interference, and your child will love "helping."

Treasure Hunt

This game is particularly fun to play outside, although it can work as an indoor event as well. Take a small plastic bucket—one that your child can comfortably carry—and head outside to explore. Let her choose objects to put in the bucket, encouraging her to pick up leaves, pluck blades of grass, and pick up stones, twigs, or handfuls of sand. Your child will love to carry (as well as dump) the bucket full of treasures, and plucking, twisting, picking, and scooping are all great ways to practice hand movements and dexterity.

HOW IT ALL FITS: SPATIAL DEVELOPMENT

All the aspects of your toddler's development are coming together in a remarkable combination of skills that result in some amazing advances in his development of spatial relations. Both his visual-spatial (determining distance, sorting shapes, recognizing patterns, and sequencing and ordering) and his motor-spatial (navigating around objects, balancing, and moving at varying speeds) skills will continue to sharpen through this year and the next. It's interesting to note that the right hemisphere of the brain, which controls self-awareness, art, music, and creativity, also controls spatial relations.

So, while your toddler's left brain is hard at work mastering language, recognizing patterns, and organizing spatial information, his right brain is helping him figure out how to negotiate the living room by walking rather than crawling. It's amazing to see how each element of your child's development is suddenly interrelating with many other elements and allowing your toddler to perceive his world in a complex way.

Helping your toddler to process all this new sensory input is as simple as making sure that the activities you do stimulate multiple senses and allow him to continue his burgeoning work in integrating all his new skills.

GAMES

Bang on a Drum All Day

You know how much your toddler loves to bang on things: pots, coffee tables, high-chair trays—whatever is available. Pounding toys, such as those on which he can use a hammer to bop pegs through round holes, are great for developing spatial relations skills. At first you will have to help him fit the colorful round pegs in their holes and perhaps lend a hand when hammering the pegs down, but before too long, your child will be happily banging away. This sim-

Your Baby's View: Making Friends

Imagine that you're assigned to a huge, complex, multi-task project at your office. For months, you've been logging an incredible number of days at the office, just gathering the necessary information and organizing it into usable forms. Everything is just now starting to make sense, and you're ready to really buckle down and master the subject matter. Once you do, you'll be ready for the big presentation.

One day, your boss comes into the office with another person. You're introduced, and your boss tells you that you'll be spending some time with this person. You say hello and maybe even register that this new coworker looks very nice. You even feel like you could like her. But you're busy. So very, very busy. And so, without making any chitchat, you return to your project.

But your coworker's busy, too. As busy as you, it seems. And so the two of you settle down to work in companionable silence. Perhaps you glance up once in a while and exchange brief smiles. Or you borrow the tape dispenser from your coworker's desk. Or lend her a pen. Maybe one day your boss takes the two of you to lunch, where you each vie

ple game combines sorting, fitting shapes into holes, developing the hand-eye coordination necessary for using a hammer to pound the peg in, learning cause and effect, and experiencing some fine sonic stimulation as well. Whew! Now that you know what he's working on, wouldn't you just rather take an aspirin for that headache instead of hiding the hammer after a morning of endless pounding?

a little for attention as you discuss your projects. Even though you don't speak much or share the workload, you feel a real camaraderie with this person; you perceive that you're like-minded individuals.

When it comes right down to it, you're glad to share space with this person. It's companionable, and you both seem to be doing the same sort of thing. Maybe one day, when you've mastered your project, the two of you can hang out together. You really do believe you've become quite fond of her.

Early social interactions between toddlers are not much different from the scenario described above. For the next year or two, your child will be perfectly happy playing *along side* his peers. Experts call this way of playing "parallel play," and it simply means that while an older child or an adult is often able to tailor an activity to draw a toddler out of his own single-minded exploration, another toddler is happy to simply share space and engage in her own pursuits.

As your toddler becomes a master of his basic language, cognitive, emotional, and motor skills, he will become more able to participate in cooperative play. In the meantime, let your child enjoy the companionship of others his age, but don't attempt to force them to play together.

Motion and Music

Turn on whatever music inspires you and your child. Dance, jump, or run in circles. Crouch down and walk like a duck, prance like a horse, tiptoe like a mouse. Let your child stretch her imagination as you work on rhythm and balance. The bonus? A nice aerobic workout for you.

Dookie Says

"I love to watch my videos. I can pick them up by my-self and I can almost work the VCR. Well, I would be able to, if I could ever get to it, but Mom and Dad have moved it behind the cabinet doors. Oh, well. I can always ask them to put on the TV for me. And I do. Over and over again—all day long. See how quiet I am? I'm not bothering the grown-ups and they can take care of all their grown-up chores. Why don't they let me watch as much as I want?"

There are any number of studies these days regarding toddlers and television watching, and as the creator of a video and DVD series, I'll be the first to say that I don't agree with the inflexible rule of absolutely no watching TV shows, DVDs, or videos, ever. In fact, there are many experts who agree with my philosophy that TV shows, DVDs, and videos can have educational value and can introduce your child to a rich fantasy world that might include talking animals, crazy puppets, or spellbinding scenery.

What is important to remember is that TV, DVD, or video viewing, like any treat, is best in moderation. And it's not bad to have a few general rules:

- Always be sure that what your child is watching is age-appropriate.

- Limit the amount of time your toddler spends watching the television.

- Set a positive example: Don't leave the television on all day in the background; don't watch your favorite show when you are playing a game with your toddler.

- Make watching a favorite DVD or video a special event. Sit together, cuddle, and talk about what you see.

Hide-and-Seek

This game is a popular way to build spatial awareness, and it's easy to play either indoors or out. It's also a great way to incorporate number concepts as you teach your child how to count to ten while someone hides.

Start by "hiding" underneath a blanket and letting your toddler "find" you. Then hide her under the blanket. Add variety and work on naming body parts by grabbing a leg or an arm. Ask "Is this a *leg* I feel under here? Is it an *arm*?" Whip the cover off to announce in a satisfied voice, "*Nope!* It's [child's name]." Simple? Sure. But a guaranteed crowd-pleaser—trust me.

As your child gets more mobile, begin by hiding in plain sight. Crouch behind a chair so part of you sticks out. Or hide behind the curtains. Or a skinny tree. Call out "Where's Mommy [or Daddy, or whomever]?" and let your toddler locate you by your voice. This will also teach her to play by calling out her own version of "Where am I?" which will (hopefully) prevent those heart-stopping moments when she manages to hide so well you really can't find her!

GET UP AND GO: GROSS MOTOR SKILLS

From being cradled in your arms, to kicking on her back in a stroller, to sitting in a bouncy seat, to sitting in a high chair, to crawling, to cruising, and now to walking, your toddler has slowly and steadily been working to get her growing body under her control. From this point on, your toddler will likely make a steady progression in mobility

Safety Watch:
Childproofing for Climbing Toddlers

There's something very enticing about things that are out of your toddler's reach. And there are more ways than you can think of to get to those things. Now that he has the ability to move around upright, combined with stacking skills—well, there's nowhere he can't go! It's your job not to stop him from working on this new climbing skill but to keep him safe while providing some places where it's safe to practice under your supervision.

Plastic climbing gyms are small and can fit even in a cramped playroom. They often have cutouts on the bottom for crawling through and a slide for a quick trip down. Outdoor play structures also provide good opportunities for climbing practice, and many parks have structures that are scaled to toddler-size.

It's important to make your home as climb-proof as possible. Favorite furniture for climbing includes: cribs, book-

and speed. And unfortunately this desire for speed is coupled with a complete disregard for her personal safety. You'll need to perfect the art of sticking close without hovering, of calmly wiping away tears and assessing damage, and, most likely, of speed-dialing your pediatrician and rattling off the status of the injury like an extra on *ER*.

Many toddlers love to participate in specially designed gym classes that include bouncing on trampolines, playing with huge swaths of parachute cloth, and swinging from shelves, chairs, coffee tables (or, for the ambitious, kitchen and dining room tables), countertops, step stools, and dressers (ever notice how the knobs are like the handholds on the rock-climbing wall at the gym?). Take a look around your house and see what needs to be done to limit dangerous climbing.

- Make sure bookcases are anchored to the wall.
- Move furniture away from windows and install window guards.
- Fold up step stools and put them away.
- Store the most rickety of chairs, for the time being.
- Leave a pile of pillows on the floor next to the crib to cushion late-night missteps.

If your toddler is an inveterate climber, you'll need to keep a close eye on him. It's not just the heights he might reach that could be dangerous, it's also the dangerous things that you may store up high, thinking they are safe, that are now within his curious reach.

bars. Look for a facility with well-padded surfaces (including the poles and beams supporting the equipment) and a staff that specializes in tiny tumblers.

This year can be a nerve-racking time as your toddler becomes proficient on her feet at all speeds. Try not to worry too much. Toddlers are incredibly resilient and fearless (they have to be!), and with your encouragement and protection will come through this developmental phase unscathed!

Games Siblings Play

Play between older siblings and toddlers must still be carefully supervised. Early walkers are still getting their balance and may be intimidated by older, faster-moving kids. Younger siblings who are now able to get into all of the "big kid" stuff may also frustrate older children. On the other hand, older children are often more than happy to take the lead, and toddlers love to imitate, so there are still many opportunities for harmonious family fun. Here are a few ideas for games that should entertain children both large and small:

- **Zookeeper.** Let your older child pretend to be a variety of zoo animals. Designate your toddler as zookeeper and give him a plastic bucket filled with toy foods. Put the older child in the crib (cage), and have the toddler make the rounds to feed the roaring lion, chattering chimp, bark-

GAMES

Olympic Gymnast

Use a long two-inch-by-four-inch board. For younger toddlers, start with encouraging them to walk on it while it lies flat on the ground. As they become older, lift the board a few inches off the floor with a stack of bricks (outside) or books (inside) to make a more challenging balance beam. Start with it turned so your toddler is walking on the wider side of the board. Hold her hands for balance and help her cross from one side to the other.

ing seal, and trumpeting elephant. Offer them a chance to reverse roles and let your toddler make the animal noises.

- **A Grand Parade.** Break out the musical instruments and noisemakers and let your older child be parade marshal and lead you and your toddler on a noisy march throughout the house or neighborhood. Wearing costumes or silly hats adds to the fun.

- **Going on a Bear Hunt.** A variation of the parade. Memorize the book *We're Going on a Bear Hunt* by Michael Rosen and Helen Oxenbury and march around the house or yard chanting and acting out the story.

- **An Evening of Theater.** Pick a favorite book that your older child knows well. Read aloud as your older child acts out the story and favorite characters. Make sure that you and your toddler offer enthusiastic applause and even a standing ovation at the end of the performance.

Magic Carpet Ride

Have your child sit on an extra-large bath or beach towel. Grab the end of the towel and *slowly* pull her across a bare floor. You can swirl her in circles, swish her from side to side, or build up to some speed on the straightaways. Just make sure that your child is ready for takeoff, or instead of happy squeals, you'll hear the *thunk* of her head bumping the floor as she tips backward off her "magic carpet."

chapter eight

Me Do This: Nineteen
through Twenty-four Months

*I*t seems like yesterday that I was helping Richard feed himself. I remember him opening his mouth, frantic for me to get that spoon in there. Sometimes I would juggle two spoons, just to make sure I had a second spoonful ready to go as soon as he gulped down the first spoonful. But now it's a whole different story. It seems like every day he grows more and more independent. I love watching him as he succeeds in accomplishing even the smallest tasks. Sometimes when he's eating and I see that it takes him a few minutes to get even one tiny pea with his fork, I try to step in and help. But every time I try to help, he says. "No, Mommy! Me do. Me do!" I appreciate this new independence in so many ways as I watch him each day. He wants to do everything himself, no help from Mommy— no matter how long it takes. And, honestly? It makes me proud.

Linda, Taylor and Richard's mom

I DID IT MY WAY

Ol' Blue Eyes may have thought he had the market cornered on independence, but over these six months you'll discover that Sinatra's got nothing on your toddler when it comes to sheer force of will. The toddler's rallying cry is "Me do!" And yet, sweetly, your toddler still needs your reassurance that it's okay to persevere at these tasks.

And your job is to stand back and let him do it. To allow your child to forge ahead in trying and mastering the skills he is acquiring, you will need the cheerful encouragement of a cheerleader, the patience of a saint, the negotiating skills of an international diplomat, and the ability to move at the speed of a three-toed sloth. In fact, the next time you are marveling at how time is passing in slow motion as you endure the endless wait required while a determined twenty-month-old dresses himself each morning, remember that allowing your child to practice simple skills will provide the stimulation that those areas of his brain need to make such tasks easy and routine.

As for what you can do about the potential embarrassment of venturing out in public with a twenty-month-old who has successfully dressed herself in an outfit of her own choosing—you're on your own. One woman I met told me her child's favorite outfit to wear outside was pajamas. I can't tell you how many times I was accompanied to the grocery store by a tutu-clad, feather-boa-flaunting, wand-waving, sparkly-red-shoe-wearing "Princess"!

As your child barrels toward her second birthday, you

may often find yourself marveling at the relatively verbal, relatively coordinated, endlessly energetic little person you have raised. During these months that go so fast, be sure to take some time to acknowledge how all the early stimulation and attention you have lavished on your child has paid off. If you really want a sense of how much your child has developed and where her early potential has taken her, turn back to the earliest chapters in this book and play with your toddler some of the games I recommended for infants. You may be surprised to see that certain games will evoke a memory and even an enthusiastic response.

Compare her reactions to the stimulation as an infant with her reaction to the games as a toddler. I'll bet you will be amazed at how sophisticated her skill levels have become. And it should be clear how the relatively simple activities that stimulated her as an infant have laid the groundwork for the more complex stimulation she now thrives on.

A STEADIER PROGRESSION

No matter how quickly your child zoomed ahead in certain areas as an infant or early toddler, as he approaches two, you may feel like he and his peers are all sort of leveling out, developmentally speaking. From the beginning of the nineteenth month to your child's second birthday, toddlers progress steadily, showing a more moderate but constant rate of development. You can expect to see a steady improvement in all areas: language, motor, cognitive, social, and emotional skills. Abstract concepts such as passage of time and emotions like empathy are beginning to develop along with social awareness and longer memory span.

Perhaps the word that best sums up your toddler over these next few months is "intense." Think of your toddler as an anthropologist studying a newly discovered tribe. You might catch her staring at you intently as you take out the dishes and set the table. Perhaps later that week you might find her setting plates down in front of her teddy bears. In fact, toddlers spend up to 20 percent of their time just watching and studying behavior. They internalize what they have observed by imitation and repetition.

Your toddler is also intent on using his developing language skills to gather more information. "Why?" or "What?" may become the most frequent word you hear. You need to acknowledge the importance of this information gathering by answering these questions each time they are asked. Even if it *is* the one-hundredth time you've explained why he shouldn't eat from the dog's dish.

Fine motor skills have improved immensely to the point where your toddler can manipulate levers, switches, and keys. This manual dexterity, combined with his unlimited interest in how things work, makes toys that "do something," like pop-ups or games where he can press buttons, very popular.

Improved physical strength and coordination let your toddler actively pursue some of the activities she sees that look so interesting. It will help if you can begin to find stimulating activities that will channel some of her physical energy.

SLEEPING AND WAKING

Your toddler's sleep needs are the same as they were in the previous six months: ten to twelve hours at night and possibly a one- to two-hour nap in the afternoon. Their growing brains and bodies need time to rest and recharge. If you have already helped your toddler learn how to drift off on his own at night, it's likely you'll have fairly smooth sailing from this point on. If your toddler has bad sleep habits or requires your attention whenever he wakes, you may be in for a stormy ride.

From about nineteen to twenty-four months, toddlers may experience interrupted sleep for several reasons: teething (second molars come in at around twenty months), night terrors, simple but significant stresses (like new babysitters, a move, a new school, or a temporarily absent parent), and trouble processing the day's events. If you've taught your child how to settle herself after waking, this brief window of disturbed sleep patterns shouldn't cause any problems down the road. If you're starting to panic as you read this and are thinking that you had better break some bad habits now, there are several parenting experts who are known for their expertise in sleep issues. Look for books by someone whose philosophy on getting toddlers to sleep most closely matches your own:

* **Jody Mindell** stresses calming, consistent routines and teaching the child how to fall asleep independently.

* **Richard Ferber** prefers consistent routines, a transitional object, and a firm emphasis on teaching children to fall asleep on their own.

* **T. Berry Brazelton** explains relaxing routines and self-comforting techniques—methods for reinforcing your toddler's growing sense of autonomy.

* **William Sears, M.D.,** teaches establishing nighttime rituals, including "parenting" by rocking her or lying down with her rather than "putting" your child to sleep.

* **Marc Weissbluth, M.D.,** offers a step-by-step program for instilling good sleep habits.

What you may have noticed in the quick summary above is that no matter what approach they take to resolving sleep issues, the experts all agree on one thing regarding toddlers and sleep: routine. A routine of any kind is important for toddlers. As your toddler struggles with her desire for independence, it is reassuring, even relaxing, to her to know what is coming next. So, particularly at bedtime, a consistent routine may mean a smoother transition from awake to asleep.

Following is the bedtime routine in our household, which has existed, in more or less the same order, for the better part of five years. Although there are a lot of steps, it's not as complicated as it seems—especially after doing it every night for five years! Once you find the right bedtime groove, you can speed through some sections while lingering over others. Don't worry: Your child will let you know if you've left anything important out! It's also a good idea (if a little controlling) to write down the bedtime routine for any babysitter or occasional caregiver.

Best Bedtime Routine

* **Go wild:** Get those giggles and wiggles out. Let your toddler run naked through the house, jump on a mattress (set on the floor, please), and generally go crazy. Join in as much as you want! Let the revelry continue for all of ten minutes, then swoop her off to the tub.

* **Soak your troubles away:** Slip your child into a relaxing warm bath. Don't encourage wild splashing play or general rowdiness (it's not safe in the tub anyway!). Use a washcloth to give a massage and cuddle her dry, rather than briskly rubbing.

* **Attend to details:** Brush teeth, put on diapers and pjs, all in a low-key manner.

* **Unwind:** Sit together and talk or play quietly. Many toddlers like to review their day before going to sleep. You can talk about what she did from the time she woke up right until going to bed. Processing the

information from the day in this way will help your toddler to relax.

* **Good night, good night, good night:** Get her ready to go to bed by wishing everyone a good night: siblings, parents, pets, favorite toys, the moon. Use your judgment in how long you want to spend on this—as your child gets older, she'll quickly figure out this is a great way to stall.

* **Story time:** Snuggle together in a big chair or on the bed and read a few books. Or, make up a story that features your child. My husband does this, and it makes him a favorite at bedtime.

* **A little night music:** Turn on some soft classical music. Of course, both my daughters loved the Baby Prodigy *Musical Pacifier* CDs!

* **Mood lighting:** The total darkness that helped your baby sleep through the night may petrify your toddler if he awakens. Use a small night-light to cast a reassuring glow.

* **Kiss and go:** Tell your child one last good night, tuck her in with a kiss, and leave without hesitating. Don't let yourself get suckered back for another kiss, or for a drink of water, or to find a missing toy.

If you linger outside your toddler's door after you've put her to sleep, you will hear her chatting away in what some parenting experts call "crib narratives." Just as you re-

Your Baby's View: Leaving the Party

Imagine you've just spent a lovely day with dear friends. It's been loads of fun, but it's getting late. You're tired and, quite frankly, ready for bed. Your friends see you to your room and wish you a good night. As you get into bed, your curiosity starts to nag at you. There's a sliver of light showing under your door, and if you listen carefully, you can hear the murmur of your friends' voices and maybe the clink of silverware. What are they doing out there? Is it a party? Why didn't they encourage you to stay? You begin to toss and turn. What, exactly, might you be missing? You think about getting out of bed, maybe you even swing your feet over the edge. But you're tired, and now maybe a little paranoid. They brought you to your room, didn't they? Left you lying here in the dark. Why don't they want you? And so you lie awake in the dark, wondering what you might be missing out on.

Every day is one big party to your toddler, and separation at nighttime can make him acutely aware that the party continues even after he's left. It will help your child to feel like he's not missing out if you can make his sleeping environment as welcoming as possible. Special sheets may make his bed more inviting, a favorite plush toy can become a bedtime companion, and a white noise machine or relaxing music can mask the distractions of other household sounds. The goal is to have your child *prefer* to stay in his bed.

Did You Know?: Nightmares and Night Terrors

As your toddler's imagination and memory grow and improve, she may begin waking at night from nightmares. Stress, illness, change, or certain medications can all provoke bad dreams. Unlike an adult, however, a toddler cannot dismiss the fearful scenes that wake her in the middle of the night as "only dreams." If your child is having nightmares that are disturbing her sleep, she will need your help to feel secure enough to go back to sleep. Make sure she feels safe, even if it means turning on the light or leaving a night-light on. Reassure her that she isn't in any danger from whatever scary creatures are haunting her sleep. Let her talk about her bad dream, especially if the memory of it is still with her in the morning.

If your child wakes you in the night with his screaming and thrashing but doesn't appear to acknowledge you when you arrive at his bedside, he may be experiencing night terrors. Don't try to wake him or restrain his flailing limbs. A

lived the day with your child as part of the bedtime routine, she will now review for herself. This reliving and interpreting of her day gives her a feeling of mastery and allows her to work out any frustrations she may have experienced.

One mother remembers how her toddler daughter would demand each night to "talk about my day." The two would sit together at bedtime, and the mother would patiently retrace each step of her daughter's day, from waking night terror should abate within ten to fifteen minutes, and your child will have no recollection of the event the next morning. Most children who experience night terrors stop having them by the time they are starting grade school— around age six.

How can you tell if your child is having a nightmare or a night terror?

- **Bad dreams** occur more frequently and during the later, lighter stage of REM (rapid eye movement) sleep. Your child will likely wake from a nightmare and may be able to describe his dream. Bad dreams are relatively brief, but your child may remain upset for a while after waking.

- **Night terrors** occur less frequently and during very deep, non-REM sleep. Your child will likely be unable to recall an episode of night terror. Your child will not be fully awake, although his eyes may be slightly open or staring. Night terrors last longer than a bad dream, and your child will likely continue to sleep once they end.

to pulling on pajamas, highlighting any particularly interesting moments. No detail was too small for her daughter to review. Once Mom had left the room, the little girl could be heard saying firmly, "Talk about my day *again*." She would then run through the same dialogue, sometimes twice. After about half an hour or forty-five minutes of chatter, there'd be complete silence and a blissfully sleeping child.

STIMULATING YOUR TODDLER

As you watch your busy toddler move through her day, it is clear what child-care experts mean when they say, "Play is a child's work." Over these next six months, your child will begin to enjoy *symbolic* play—feeding her dolls, making a "house" out of blocks, causing two stuffed animals to carry on a conversation. This symbolic play grows out of your child's study of you and her desire to imitate behaviors.

Imitative play is still important. Your toddler learns by helping, and you can enhance his experience by making such learning fun. Let your toddler practice fine motor skills by turning on the faucets and "washing" plastic dishes and cups while you make dinner. Give him a child-sized broom or vacuum cleaner and have him help you clean house. Show him how he can water plants by pouring from a small pitcher, or teach him how to hang up his clothes on easy-to-reach pegs. Give him a doll and let him take care of his "baby" throughout the day.

As she approaches age two, your child will become more and more confident in her large motor skills. Give her plenty of opportunities to challenge her growing sense of balance on her feet. She is probably already proficient at crawling up stairs; now is the time to teach her how to creep down backward. Your child will still love music and the opportunity to dance. Use music as a background for any kind of movement games. Help your child tune in to the different rhythms around her: knocking on doors, clapping in patterns, hammering on pegboards.

Your toddler is also ready, willing, and able to begin to

play with others. While much of her play in her second year will be parallel play, which I discussed in the previous chapter, she will definitely benefit from regular social interactions with her peers.

Conversation becomes a two-way street during these months, and your child will usually understand simple commands. You can help her link these commands to concepts through repetition and visual clues. Urgently saying, "Don't touch! The stove is hot. It will hurt your hand," while shaking your head and making sure your facial expressions register great concern will have much more of an impact than saying, "No. Stop that this instant."

The clearer you can be in your communication, the easier it will become to instill discipline and a willingness to listen. Although, as your child gains more and more of a sense of independence, she may decide that obeying what she hears is not a priority. By around eighteen months, your child is developing an independent basic sense of right and wrong.

You may even see glimmers of self-discipline. I would often hear my daughter Lara saying, "No. No. No," to herself. I soon learned to check on her whenever I heard her saying "No," as it usually meant she was in the process of doing—or about to do—something she knew she shouldn't.

TODDLER STEPS

From the beginning of the nineteenth month to his second birthday, your toddler will be steadily linking multiple skills in increasingly sophisticated ways. An activity as sim-

Dookie Says

"My friend is coming over today. Mommy says we're going to play. But when he gets here, he just takes all my toys. Look! He's got my favorite car. When I grab it from him, he gets mad and pushes me. When he tries to play with my car—it's my favorite—he puts his hand too close to my mouth. So I bite it! Now everyone is telling me 'Bad.' And he's the one who took my car. I'm not sure this 'playing' is such a great idea."

As he approaches his second birthday, your toddler is certainly ready to begin to spend time with other children his age. But it is important not to lose sight of the fact that for your nineteen- to twenty-four-month-old, there is only one person who counts: him. In fact, most toddlers are not really ready for cooperative group play until they are three or older. Here are a few things you can do to begin to help your child learn how to behave when he's having a playdate, and it won't be long until he learns how to be happily engaged in sharing and playing with a friend or two.

ple as building a tower of blocks involves not just the gross motor skills to go and get the blocks off the shelf, or the verbal skills to ask you for his blocks, but also the manual dexterity to pick up the blocks, the visual-spatial relation to decide which to stack, and the hand-eye coordination to place one on top of the other.

As he did from his twelfth to eighteenth months, your toddler will continue to develop at his own rate, surging ahead in some areas and progressing more slowly in others.

Playdate Strategies:

- **Set a good example.** Make sure you are on your best behavior. Model good manners (say please and thank you), smile, and use a pleasant voice. Take turns.

- **Don't force togetherness.** Two toddlers enjoying different but similar activities in the same room defines a successful playdate at this age.

- **Don't interfere.** If the two friends are "working something out," I generally try to stay out of the picture unless physical harm seems imminent.

- **Do have duplicate toys.** If your child has a favorite toy, keep a duplicate on hand that can come out during playdates. At this age, similar but different isn't better and sharing isn't an option. If you're going to play with balls, it's better to have two red balls than one red and one blue.

- **Have a snack at the ready.** A little treat can go a long way in promoting togetherness and preventing hunger-induced crankiness.

As you look at the list below, consider whether your child is making consistent progress in any given area.

Of course, if you have any questions or concerns at all about your child's rate of development, you should consult your pediatrician.

Somewhere between the end of the nineteenth month and his second birthday, your child should have achieved the milestones listed in the previous chapter, as well as those listed below. He should be able to:

* "feed" a doll or stuffed animal
* wash his hands
* speak clearly and be understood by others
* brush his teeth (with help)
* put on a piece of clothing
* put on shoes
* jump up off the ground
* stand on one foot if holding onto something
* carry on an understandable conversation
* identify friends by name

TODDLER TALK

Many toddlers just shy of two years old use simple sentences with verbs and may be beginning to add adverbs or adjectives. But even if your toddler isn't a chatterbox, she may already be communicating at levels above those of her more verbose peers. The use of gestural speech is considered by some experts to be the most reliable indicator of your toddler's understanding of the rules of communication. If your child is able to use her body and gestures to clearly communicate language, she is likely on the verge of bursting forth with a torrent of words.

Your toddler is constantly working on his speech development. One of the most important ways you can help your child improve his communication skills is by continuing to support a running dialogue throughout your day. Always make sure you allow him plenty of chances to initiate a conversation, even if his first attempts are nonverbal.

The conversations your toddler has on her own are also

important in helping her to understand the role of language in interpreting actions and events. In the book *Narratives from the Crib,* Dr. Katherine Nelson analyzed the monologues of a typical toddler when left alone in her crib. She theorized that these monologues are not simply practice of word mastery but an attempt to make sense of daily experiences.

As your child's speech becomes more fluid, he launches into the next stage of language development, which is not simply using words as labels but beginning to address concepts and express his thought processes. As your child starts to use language in a more sophisticated way, you will encounter some examples of what I call "toddler grammar"— a use of grammar that makes perfect logical sense, while not exactly following recognized grammatical rules. For instance:

* **Subject-verb relationship.** If your toddler wants to go with Daddy to the store, he may say "Go Daddy?" If he knows that Daddy is going to the store, he may state, "Daddy go."

* **Plurals.** What could be easier? Just add an "s" at the end of a word to indicate more. Like "mouses" or "foots" or "tooths."

* **Past tenses.** Past tense is created by adding a "d." Your toddler may say things like "I goed" or "Kitty eated."

It's important that you do not discourage these early attempts at complex language. As your toddler struggles to make sense of the English language's admittedly complex grammar structure, you can help him by offering quick and understanding responses that keep him interested in continuing to communicate his thoughts. Make sure you answer him using proper grammar. Eventually, he will begin to pick up on the grammatical nuances.

Singing, reading, and reciting nursery rhymes are all still important ways of stimulating your toddler's developing language skills. Create stories about things you see every day, encourage your child to repeat simple rhymes along with you, and let her hold the book and turn the pages as you finish reading each one.

GAMES

I Wonder, I Wonder

Make up stories about everyday objects and people. For instance, if you are going for a stroll to the park and see a dog walking on a leash, start a story with "I wonder where the dog is going?" Your younger child may simply turn and look at the dog expectantly; your older toddler may answer something like "Park." Pick up the story from your child's cue. "Yes, the dog is on his way to the park. When he gets there, he will chase a ball and run and play. What will we do at the park?" This kind of dialogue stimulates both conversational and imaginative skills.

The Name Game (Reprise)

In chapter 3, I talked about how your very tiny baby was interested in labeling things. That interest enjoys a resurgence, and this time your toddler loves to do the naming herself. Add another element by using a descriptive word for things you are naming. For instance, when setting the table, show your child a plate and say, "Here is a blue . . ." Pause and let her shout out "Plate!" Then hold up another and say "And here is a red . . ." Before you know it, your child will be jumping in to add the adjective as well as the noun.

Life as a Musical

Make even the most mundane tasks enjoyable, by encouraging your toddler to sing along with you as you set basic sentences to song. Getting dressed in the morning becomes a whole new enterprise when you sing (to the tune of "Farmer in the Dell"): "We're putting on your shirt. We're putting on your shirt. Hi, ho, here we go! We're putting on your shirt [and pants, and socks, and shoes]." Other great tunes to use include: "Twinkle, Twinkle, Little Star," "She'll Be Coming 'Round the Mountain," or "I've Been Working on the Railroad." Use your imagination and transform a trip to the grocery store into a Broadway show.

THE LITTLE THINGS: FINE MOTOR SKILLS

By now your child has increasingly skilled manual dexterity and wants to try to perform tasks using her fingers and hands. She may insist on getting herself dressed, making food, or trying to pour her juice. While she can't always do everything she wants to do easily, it is important that you remain encouraging. Be creative and find ways that let her

Monkey Hear, Monkey Say

Here's a small but important reminder: Watch what you say within earshot of your toddler! He is constantly on the lookout for new words to add to his vocabulary. If you slip up and let something out that you wish you hadn't, don't make a big fuss, even if he tries repeating it one or two times. Remember, *any* kind of attention is good attention as far as your toddler is concerned. I myself have managed to prune my strong language down to a fierce *"Darn it!"*

Even if it feels strange at first, I think you'll find that it's not so difficult to adapt to G-rated speech. But I will admit it raises an eyebrow—and has been known to induce a smirk or two—when, in attempting to get my point across in the midst of a heated discussion with adults, I feel compelled to use one of my kid-friendly "expletives."

be successful at the tasks she attempts: choose outfits with large, loopy buttonholes, give her a measuring cup full of cereal and let her pour it into the bowl. Then use a tiny pitcher and teach her how to pour liquids into a cup (two-handed works best!).

Between the ages of eighteen and twenty-four months, your toddler is also likely to become very interested in drawing or scribbling or other forms of artistic expression. Your budding artist is exercising both his fine motor skills and his visual acumen with these early works of squiggles, lines, and dots as he learns that he is able to control his hand to create particular visual patterns. Experts categorize the early phases of working with crayon and paper as "disordered scribbling" and "controlled scribbling." Both of these stages of exploration are more about the control of motion than anything else, so your toddler will like working with a dark crayon on large sheets of paper that are taped securely to the floor or table. That way he can concentrate on the connection between movement of his hand and what appears on the paper. Different colors of crayon can add additional stimulation.

Your toddler will enjoy many kinds of manipulative art over these next few months. Clay, finger painting, painting with a brush, using stamps, drawing, and cutting and sticking all encourage exploration in different mediums.

GAMES

Costume Box

Toddlers love dress-up, and easy-to-slip-on clothing lets them practice dressing themselves while engaging in imaginative play. Capes, smocks, long scarves (supervise carefully if she is wrapping it around her neck), tutus, aprons, large pieces of fabric with slits (like ponchos), vests, and hats, hats, hats are all easy for your toddler to put on herself. Both boys and girls will enjoy creating costumes and dressing up. Be sure not to discourage creativity. If your son wants to wear a tutu, let him go for it!

Mixed-media Artists

Let your toddler explore his love of drawing and painting in a variety of ways. Use food coloring to tint shaving

Bookshelf

Books should continue to be a big part of your toddler's life. Sturdy board books will let an independent child easily turn the pages by herself. Old magazines, especially toy catalogs, can provide hours of "reading" fun and are great for launching discussions. It's likely that your child will attach herself to a favorite story. After raising two toddlers, I have lost count of how many times I've read *Goodnight Moon* over the years. Trips to the library or bookstore, where a variety of books can be reviewed to see what might capture your toddler's interest, can be both fun and helpful in breaking her out of the "read it again" rut.

There are so many wonderful, exciting books for toddlers that it's hard to recommend specific titles. Choosing books to share with your toddler becomes a personal experience. But if you're stuck for ideas, ask your friends for suggestions or visit a website like Amazon.com and take a look

cream or even whipped cream and let him spread it around. (It looks like marbled paper when it dries.) Color grains of rice with food coloring, then spread a thin layer of glue on a piece of paper and let him sprinkle on a design. Buy finger paints for the tub. Or let him paint with his feet. Make sure you use washable, water-based paints. Some parenting books suggest you allow your child to finger paint with different foods or juices. Personally, I never wanted to encourage either of my daughters to play with her food, but I can see the appeal of creating an edible work of art!

at some of the lists of books enjoyed by other parents. There are also books that recommend other books, such as Kathleen Odean's *Great Books for Babies and Toddlers* and *How to Get Your Child to Love Reading* by Esmé Raji Codell. The list below includes some tried-and-true books that my girls have loved.

- *Good Night, Gorilla* by Peggy Rathmann
- Any Dr. Suess book, especially *The Cat in the Hat, Green Eggs and Ham,* and *Fox in Socks*
- *Owl Babies* by Martin Waddell and Patrick Benson
- *Jesse Bear, What Will You Wear?* by Nancy White Carlstrom
- *Go Dog, Go!* by Philip D. Eastman
- *Chicka Chicka Boom Boom* by Bill Martin, Jr.
- *What Mommies Do Best/What Daddies Do Best* by Laura Numeroff Joffe

A Penny Saved ...

This is a game that needs to be played under close supervision to ensure no coins are swallowed. Find a plastic jar or container with a fairly wide mouth and neck. Give your toddler a pile of pennies and let her drop them into the jar. Add water and a lid and slosh the pennies around. Talk about how heavy the jar becomes. Empty the jar, refill it with water, and drop in the pennies one by one until the water overflows. Simple experiments like these allow your child to practice motor skills while learning simple lessons in cause and effect.

Left- or Right-Handedness

Only 5 to 10 percent of the general population favors their left hand, and scientists theorize that the trait of left- or right-handedness is genetically determined. When both parents are lefties, their child is more than 50 percent likely to also be a lefty. When one parent is left-handed, the likelihood drops to about 17 percent, and when both parents favor their right hands, their child has only a 2 percent chance of being left-handed. In any case, toddlers don't usually decide on a dominant hand until after age three, and in fact many children at this age are equally proficient with their left and right hands.

No Greater Gift

Your toddler will love to unwrap things. Start out by wrapping favorite toys or books. Don't use too much tape or complicated ribbons and knots. You can wrap with newspaper, tissue, or recycled wrapping paper. In fact, the presentation of the "gift" is beside the point. Your child will love the discovery that comes with uncovering the object itself.

HOW IT ALL FITS: SPATIAL DEVELOPMENT

As your toddler's spatial development continues to grow more sophisticated over these next six months, the activities you do together can become increasingly complex. As you watch your child attempt to master a new skill, you

Dottie Says

"I love to draw so much. I'm quite a good artist. I scribble and scribble. And I have the nicest crayons. Everyone says I'm very talented. But the other day, I was just finishing an extensive mural on my bedroom wall when Mom walked in. And I have to say, she didn't seem pleased at all. In fact, she scrubbed my work right off the wall. I don't know what's wrong. I thought she loved my coloring."

It's bound to happen at least once: Your aspiring artist will suddenly turn graffiti artist. If you discover that your walls have been redecorated, first take a deep breath and count to ten. Your toddler doesn't know she's done anything wrong, and you don't want to squelch her creativity by yelling at her or punishing her. You need to help her understand that there are appropriate places to draw. If you catch her in the middle of the act, pull out a piece of paper and redirect her to it. Let her finish her project and then explain that walls are not for drawing on. Give her a towel and let her help you clean the wall. Then show her how you can hang art that's been done on paper on the wall for the same effect. If she persists in decorating your walls, you may want to invest in a standing easel. It may be that she prefers to work standing up.

can know that he is working hard at bringing to bear on a particular task all the separate pieces of his development.

Given the "Me do!" nature of your toddler as she approaches her second birthday, you may not be so surprised when I tell you that one of the best kinds of stimulation you can offer is letting her figure things out on her own. For instance, if she's working on one of those wooden puzzles where pictures of animals or other objects are taken out and replaced in spaces with a matching picture, she may immediately know *where* a particular piece belongs (good visual skills) but may have trouble fitting the piece into the space in exactly the right way (developing fine motor skills). Let her try to fit the piece in the correct spot. But be sure to lend a hand before frustration ruins the fun of the new challenge. At this age, a bit of a challenge can be good—as long as your child can feel she has succeeded.

So whether your child is exploring sequencing by lining up a row of different-sized blocks or fitting together a nesting toy, or is working on hand-eye coordination by attempting to make a straight line on paper or put a puzzle piece in place, or accurately using his spoon to get a mouthful of oatmeal, you need to let him try on his own. Be encouraging, and learn to know when to step in and offer the support that will let him be successful at his efforts.

Many of the games I've suggested to enhance fine and gross motor skills are also naturally conducive to developing your toddler's spatial skills. As you may have surmised, by around age two, your child will benefit most from stimulation that does not simply concentrate on one discrete area but requires him to use multiple skills in concert.

GAMES

Tennis, Anyone?

Using your hands (for younger toddlers) and plastic spatulas (for older), bat a Mylar balloon back and forth. To make it more challenging, put an obstacle between you and your child and try to get the balloon from one side to the other. If this game occasionally starts to resemble golf more than tennis as your toddler swats the balloon once it lands on the ground, don't worry. It's the same idea. Besides, two words: Tiger Woods.

Discovery Table

You can buy fancy tables just like they use in preschools, or you can simply get a long, shallow plastic container (with a lid is best) and place it on a low table. Fill the container with cotton balls, or rice, or kernels of corn, or sand, or water and let your child decide how to use it. He may make roads for his cars in the sand, or experiment with what will float or sink in water. Toddlers love to poke and twist and mash, so fill the box with a dough (real or a Play-Doh™ mixture that has been tinted with food coloring) and let him pretend to make bread or pizza. Use your imagination and find new ways for your toddler to explore dimension and texture. Let him squeeze and twist, and build things up and knock them down. And when he's done, just pop the lid on the container and store it until the next time.

Button, Button, Who's Got the Button?

Let your toddler develop her visual memory and problem-solving skills by playing this game with three large plastic

Toy Chest

Since your toddler is continuing to develop both intellectually and physically over these months, you need to offer toys that will stimulate your child's expanding range of talents and interests. Toys like baby dolls or miniature kitchen sets that allow toddlers to imitate grown-up life can promote imaginative play and motor skills. Toys of varying shapes or sizes stimulate developing spatial skills. Toys with buttons or levers that, when manipulated, cause motion or reveal something provide both an opportunity to work on manual dexterity and early lessons in cause and effect. Art supplies promote creativity and experimentation. Riding and pushing toys challenge increasingly sophisticated gross motor skills.

Make sure that the toys you choose are age-appropriate. Toys that are too difficult for your toddler to operate will be frustrating at best and dangerous at worst. Pick toys that are in line with your child's interests. If he's passionate about dinosaurs, look for puzzles with a dino theme or for plastic dinosaurs that he can manipulate. If you have a daughter who loves dolls, get a doll stroller, a bottle, and some simple items of clothing so she can fully "take care" of her baby.

cups and an object small enough to fit under them. (Don't actually use a button, though. The object should not be so small that it poses a choking hazard.) Turn the three cups over, with one covering the object. Encourage your child to point to one of the cups, and then lift it up to reveal whether or not the object is there. As she becomes more

If you get a toy that seemed great in the store but is too challenging for your toddler, wait until he has lost interest and simply store the toy for future exploration. He'll be ready for it before you know it.

At this age, toy stores can be a treat for both children and adults. Here's a list of a few things that will make great playthings for the next few months and probably over the next few years:

- play kitchen set with real or plastic food
- toddler tape player and tapes
- puppets (finger puppets are easier for younger toddlers; older children may be able to manipulate hand puppets). Old socks, when decorated, can make great puppets!
- alphabet or number blocks
- large building block systems
- shape sorters
- sand boxes and sand toys
- dolls and accessories
- noise-making instruments like tambourines, maracas, drums, or xylophones

skilled at remembering which cup hides the object, slowly shuffle the cups around. Letting her lift the cup to reveal the object adds another dimension to this game. We do this exact same demo in the first Baby Prodigy video.

GET UP AND GO: GROSS MOTOR SKILLS

As your adventurous, physical toddler continues to push the limits of physical space, you may notice a period where he slows down or suddenly refuses to participate in a rough-and-tumble game he once enjoyed. One mom remembers how her son, who used to be a terror on the playground slide, suddenly refused to both climb up and slide down. It wasn't until she learned that while out with a babysitter, he'd gone zooming down the slide, only to land firmly and probably painfully on his butt, that she understood his reluctance to return to his daredevil tactics on the playground.

Your toddler's increasing capability to remember events and to link cause and effect may now cause him to become intimidated or even fearful. As much as you want to safeguard your toddler, you should not become overprotective or try to discourage his adventurousness. It's a fine line you'll need to walk for the next few months, or even year.

Your toddler is on a path of increasing coordination and confidence. Over the past six months you encouraged and challenged your child to safely test his skills against new obstacles. You should continue to look for ways to stimulate his gross motor coordination in combination with other developing skills. Use the games below as suggestions for how to incorporate other skills along with climbing, running, and balancing.

Safety Watch: Covering the Basics

Now that your toddler is a better communicator, you can begin the incredibly important project of teaching him some basic safety lessons. Start now and repeat them often, and eventually your warnings will take hold. As the parent of any toddler knows, the most innocent places or activities can be fraught with danger for your mobile disaster magnet. I could fill a whole chapter with items or situations that are potentially dangerous to your toddler, but instead I offer the list below simply as a starting point for you to develop your own safety program for your toddler to follow.

Teach the dangers of:

- sharp or pointy
- hot
- stairs
- electrical outlets or cords
- tubs, pools, or other bodies of water
- small items that don't belong in the mouth
- poisonous substances (houseplants, medicines, "grown-up" drinks like coffee or alcohol)
- traffic
- pets (your own and strange animals)

Games Siblings Play

As you approach the two-year mark with your toddler, I hope that your children have settled into a routine of enjoying each other's company. Of course, I can pretty much promise you that your older child will sometimes feel claustrophobic or irritated by the attentions of her younger sibling. And that your toddler will generally consider himself his sister's biggest fan—or stalker.

While appreciating that some private time for each child will be both appreciated and necessary, you can continue to create opportunities for mutually satisfying play.

- **Lion Tamer.** Hugely popular in our household. One person (usually me) got to be the lion tamer. Everyone else was a lion. I would command my beasts up onto couches and footstools. Have them sit up, beg, roll over, and roar. Both my children would completely get into the spirit of

GAMES

Catch It on a Bounce, Catch It on the Fly

Use a large rubber ball and let your child practice catching it after one bounce. Call out "Bounce" before sending it her way. The next time, gently lob the ball underhand, calling out "Fly." Encourage your child to call out "Bounce" or "Fly" before sending the ball back to you. Begin the game by standing just a step or two apart. As you get better, take steps backward and increase the distance between you. This game combines language, anticipation, and hand-eye things—so much so that, even when I was done, two little "lions" would continue to roam around the house.

- **Follow the Leader.** Have a slightly bossy older child in the house? Here's the perfect chance for her to tell her little brother or sister just what to do—and have the satisfaction of watching the younger child do it. With younger toddlers, supervise to make sure that the older child doesn't do anything that is unsafe for either child.

- **Pop Bottle Bowling.** Use empty two-liter bottles and a large rubber ball. A narrow hallway makes an excellent bowling alley. Teach your toddler how to roll the ball by swinging it from between his legs (a "diaper roll") as opposed to a sidearm roll. Numbering the bottles from one to ten can be a good way to let the older child keep score by either adding up the numbers on the bottles standing (lowest score wins) or the numbers on the fallen bottles (highest score wins). It's also a great way to introduce numbers to your toddler.

coordination. You may wonder how it works the larger motor skills. Those skills come into play as you both chase after all of the bounces or flys that you miss!

Red Light, Green Light, Yellow Light

A classic game with an added twist. As you know, red light means "stop," green means "go," and yellow means "hop!" For a younger child, you'll play the game while keeping an eye on him as he learns to make his body match your commands. As he gets older, you can turn your back after you say green, and spin around as you say red. Make sure you pause after saying "Red" and use your body language to give him a clue as to when you are going to turn around.

Walk Like a Duck

Or hop like a frog, or trot like a horse, or skitter like a mouse, or sway like an elephant. Adding animal noises makes this game even more fun. Remember to let your child have a chance to take the lead and decide what kind of creatures you will be.

chapter nine

The Preschool Years:
Two Years and Beyond

How exciting it has been to watch our daughter develop over the last two years. We have loved watching her reach all of her developmental milestones. My husband and I have also reached our own parental milestones. We've taught our daughter, and she's taught us, too. Now, as she enters into the preschool years, we are excited to continue to learn and grow with her. I am also proud to say that I have learned so much about myself through my daughter and have become not only a better parent, but also a better person. I have cherished every moment and will always remember the first time she smiled, the first word she said, and the first steps she took. I look forward to her next steps in growing and learning as well as our next steps as parents.

Lindsay, Casey's mom

MOVIN' ON

I spent my daughter's second birthday in sort of a daze. Not because I couldn't figure out where two years had flown, although that was surely part of it, but because the little baby I had struggled with in our hospital room as I tried to dress her in her little homecoming outfit was now a walking, talking marvel of a child.

I was proud as I watched her "host" her first party, greeting the friends who had arrived at the teddy bear tea, pouring cups of juice from a tiny pitcher, playing a rousing game of pin the tail on the donkey, and gleefully unwrapping her presents. And I was amazed, too. In simple ways that were nonetheless remarkable to me, she was able to nearly seamlessly integrate all the skills that I had watched her develop over the past years.

She had grown so much. And I had enjoyed helping her to reach this point. In fact, as I let her help me slice her birthday cake, I was already starting to look forward to the amazing growth and development to come.

THE NEXT LEVEL

Your child has passed through infancy and through toddlerhood and is now on the threshold of his preschool years. His brain is still growing and increasing in density. In some ways, his ability to learn and your ability to influence his happiness and intelligence is no different from how it was when he was born. Each experience he has still plays a role in strengthening existing neuronal connections or continuing to pave new ones. But as he moves into his third year of life, your child has gone beyond practicing simple fine and gross motor skills and mastering basic language functions. He is now working on developing increasingly more sophisticated types of cognitive, social, and emotional responses.

As intimidating as this may sound, I want to reassure you that you do not have to do anything different from what you've been doing all along: providing your child with stimulation that is appropriate to his temperament and ability. The good foundations for learning and developing, which you have helped your child to form from infancy until now, can help to make this next step in his growth lots of fun for both of you.

Stimulating your preschool child is as intensive an undertaking as introducing your newborn to her world. It would take another book to fully discuss the developmental stages from preschool to kindergarten. But I wanted to give you a peek at what sort of developments lie ahead and offer you a perspective from which to observe, and participate in, this next stage in your child's life.

HOW AND WHAT PRESCHOOLERS ARE LEARNING

Your child has been learning from you since the day she was born and will continue to learn from you whether or not you are always conscious of teaching her. At the early preschool stage, there is still not much distinction between playing and learning. In fact, think of play as an activity your child engages in as a way of learning.

From learning her cues in infancy to picking up on clues in toddlerhood, you have learned what your child needs and wants. In these early preschool years, the best way to provide ongoing stimulation is to let your child continue to lead you. If you follow her interests and continue to expose her to new experiences, you will be teaching her on a daily basis. In the preceding chapters, the stimulation you provided your baby and toddler was aimed at enhancing basic, developing skills. With your preschooler, that attention has paid off. The interactions, stimulation, and experiences you provide in the following areas can be more sophisticated and still fun!

LANGUAGE

The thrill you experienced when your baby uttered her first word may turn to frustration as she can now use language in ways that may exasperate you. Stammering or stuttering, using baby talk, chattering nonstop, picking up "naughty" words or experiencing the power of "bathroom talk," using angry words (the first "I hate you" is an arrow to any parent's heart but an inevitable wound)—all these variations of the power of language will be explored by your preschooler.

What is truly exciting about your preschooler's increasing mastery of language is she can now begin to use language not just to talk about what is going on around her, but to express things that are in her head. Language continues to develop at a phenomenal pace during the preschool years, especially in the following ways:

* use of pronouns
* ability to question: What? Why?
* using words to control personal behavior
* using words to control other's behavior
* using words to boost self-esteem or ask for approval
* using words to express abstract ideas

FINE MOTOR SKILLS

Your child's mastery of fine motor skills opens the door to all kinds of experiences during her preschool years. She will be able to dress herself, to help you cook by stirring and mixing—or even cracking the eggs—and to draw or use art materials with increasing creativity. Observe your child carefully and always be ready to offer her a chance to try her skills at a new activity. Even if she is not successful at first, with practice and encouragement she will quickly master new tasks. Your child's increased manual dexterity means that she is also ready for simple instruction on musical instruments *if she remains enthusiastic about the lessons.*

You may notice that as your child moves into her preschool years, she will abandon some of the toys you purchased to promote her fine motor skills. Puzzles or games with knobs and buttons may lose their appeal when stacked up against something as interesting as sorting the silverware into the right compartments in the drawer or helping you roll the socks in the laundry.

Many preschoolers do become interested in playing card games. This is an activity that is good for their fine motor skills, as well as their newly forming interest in numbers.

Gross Motor Skills

Just as your toddler pushed the physical limits of his body in all his activities, your preschooler will continue to learn how to use his body in ways that are both fun and practical. During the preschool years, your child may begin to acquire the physical skills that will distinguish him as an athletic adult. Playing ball, swimming, taking dance classes, mastering the balance and strength needed to ride a tricycle, learning to ski, even playing basic games like tag and hopscotch—all these activities will enhance his endurance, balance, and confidence.

Spatial Relations

Your child will begin to express more sophisticated concepts of spatial relations through language, using abstract ideas like in front of, behind, or beside. Her understanding of spatial relations in combination with her visual skills will gradually become apparent as her artwork becomes more representational and sophisticated.

NEW CHALLENGES AND NEW OPPORTUNITIES

Although your preschooler has mastered an impressive number of skills, his learning process is still racing ahead as his brain continues to grow at a phenomenal rate throughout his third year. And while he may be confidently using language and boldly displaying his physical skills, there are new areas where proper stimulation can help promote learning, satisfaction, and confidence. Here's a quick preview of areas where providing the right kind of stimulation can make your preschooler happier and smarter.

EARLY EDUCATION

While no child who is being nurtured and stimulated at home *needs* to attend preschool, a quality preschool program can offer your child a wide range of experiences. By the age of three, some children are ready for the more formal structure of a preschool. Look for a preschool with quality, highly trained instructors and a philosophical approach to learning that mirrors your own.

Preschools can be based on any one or a combination of philosophies. The list below is a sampling of what philosophies you might find as you begin to research preschool options in your area. This list was drawn from www.parentspress.com/edupreschooltypes.html, which also offers a brief definition of each philosophy:

* Montessori
* Waldorf
* Reggio Emilia
* developmental
* Bank Street
* parent co-operative
* play-based
* High/Scope
* academic
* religious

Experts generally agree on the advantages of pre-school—for instance, the opportunity to play with a group of other children of the same age, formal and age-appropriate lessons, and the chance to use lots of toys and equipment you may not have at home. You may benefit from having a form of child care outside your home that is more reliable than a caregiver who does not have a substitute in case of illness or unexpected absence.

Are there disadvantages to sending your child to pre-school? Well, your child will risk a greater exposure to germs, and may spend part of his first year coming down with more illnesses than you can imagine (particularly if he is an only child and has not had a lot of exposure to common colds and child ailments). He may have to be toilet trained (a whole other book, believe me!). A program that is too academically rigorous for your child can lead to stress and burnout. You will have less flexibility in scheduling the time you spend with your child. And the cost may be prohibitive for some families.

If you decide that you or your child is not ready for the preschool experience, you can provide much of the same benefits at home. Here are some basic guidelines that offer the same kinds of stimulation and enrichment as preschool classes:

* Spend at least thirty minutes a day in conversation with your child. Give him your undivided attention and listen carefully to what he says. (Mind you, this is not thirty *consecutive* minutes—what preschooler would ever hold still for that?)

* Read to your child every day.

* Turn playtime into learning time, incorporating counting and the naming of colors, letters, and shapes into your play. Always be on the lookout for teaching moments.

* Create a routine for your child to follow. Help him to be orderly and on time.

* Help your child learn to express herself appropriately. Stress using words instead of physical acts such as hitting; stress listening instead of screaming.

* Limit TV viewing. When you do watch something (together), pick an educational program geared toward preschoolers.

* Explore your community. Take field trips to the library, the fire station, museums, or zoos.

* Allow for plenty of outside time.

* Make sure your child has chances to spend time with other children his age.

* Purchase preschool level workbooks, available at major retail chain stores.

Emergent Literacy

The term "emergent literacy" refers to behaviors that precede reading and writing and that develop into conventional literacy. "Reading" the pictures in a book and memorizing the meaning of certain shapes slowly become the recognition and retention of the meaning of symbols. Your preschooler doesn't need to be able to know what the letters S-T-O-P mean if he understands that a red octagon with those letters printed in white means "Stop." Once that association is made, it's simply a matter of time before he doesn't need the symbol to trigger the memory of what that particular arrangement of letters means. And suddenly he's on the way to reading. Think of your preschooler who is learning early reading skills as a code breaker. Encourage him to decode symbols, labels, book covers. Label familiar objects with easy-to-read flash cards. Respond positively and encouragingly, as you help him to notice that letters are a part of each of the symbols he recognizes.

One mother shamefacedly admits that her two-and-a-half-year-old son could recognize a Dunkin' Donuts sign from miles down the road. She swears that it was from going through the drive-through for coffee, but I have my suspicions! In any case, it wasn't long before he was pointing to the letter "D" and saying, "Donut!" From there it was a short step to recognizing that "D" was a part of lots of other words. Because of his good visual/memory skills, her little boy got an early start on literacy and was reading chapter books just after his third birthday.

Reading to your child promotes the "behavior" of reading. You may notice that your preschooler is sitting and "reading" to himself. It doesn't matter that the book he's holding is *Goodnight Moon* and the story that he's telling is *Peter Rabbit*. He is making an important connection between the act of reading and the story.

Scribbling is also an important part of emergent literacy. Encourage your preschooler to "write" as much as he wants (on the appropriate surfaces, of course). Between ages three and four, preschoolers may become very interested in learning how to form letters. Use refrigerator magnets of the letters of the alphabet to hold a sheet of paper to a metal baking tray and let your toddler trace the outlines of the letter. With as little pressure as possible, help guide his hand so that his scribbles begin to resemble the letters he is trying to make. (Often the letters of his name.)

This is an exciting phase of development for both you and your child. Take care not to push your child too hard in this area, or you may risk spoiling her enthusiasm for this new undertaking. She will have years ahead of her in school during which to perfect her reading and writing skills. For now, her sense of achievement is closely linked to her enjoyment of the process.

MATH AND NUMBER UNDERSTANDING

Your preschooler may already know how to count to ten, rattling off the numbers through rote memory learning. What he will begin to do over time is connect the words from one to ten to the fact that they represent numbers of *things*. You can help him make this connection by making counting a part of your day. Count stairs, count crackers, or count the birds sitting on the telephone wires. Look for age-appropriate puzzles or games, like dominoes (often you can find a child's version with animals or other objects in place of the traditional dots).

MAKING FRIENDS

Vital lessons in taking turns, sharing, and cooperation are learned throughout the preschool years. And as anyone who has watched a group of three-year-olds on a playground knows, these lessons are not always easily absorbed. Your child may need to understand that biting, kicking, or other aggressive behavior is wrong. She may need help in respecting other children's feelings. Your child still needs to be closely supervised in social settings. Getting along with other children is as much a learning experience as any of the other skills she has mastered over the past two years.

TEACHING GOOD BEHAVIOR

The behavior your child exhibited while a toddler, as acceptable as it might have been within your own family, will need to conform to the expectations of the wider world she is venturing into. There are many, many books on effective parental techniques for disciplining children, and I mention a few of them in the appendix.

I don't really like the term "discipline." When it's not put in its proper context, it can seem overly harsh. Instead of punishing my children to teach a lesson or expecting unquestioning obedience in the first place, what I tried to do was to instill in them a sense of self-discipline. And really, although it's a long process to teach a toddler or preschooler about self-discipline, in the end it really made my job as a parent much easier. Here are a few suggestions for modeling good behavior for your child:

* Reward good behavior, not bad.
* Take the positive approach.
* Be clear in your instruction—really, overly clear.
* Always take the time to explain why.
* "Do not" is for hard and fast rules only.
* Trust that your child's intentions are good.
* Admit it when you are wrong.
* Be consistent.

ROUTINE

For your toddler and now preschooler, routines offer a sense of security and control. When your child can anticipate what is coming next, she can often make transitions more smoothly. And for you, routines can be time-saving. Different families have different ways of structuring schedules. Settle on routines and rituals that are easy for you to maintain. Remember, the point of a particular routine is to make life less stressful for both you and your child. When analyzing the shape of your preschooler's day, consider if having a set way of doing things might be helpful. To get you thinking, here's a short list of activities that are easy to build routines around:

* morning wake-up and dressing
* leaving for school or work
* mealtimes
* bath and other hygiene
* cleanup
* bedtime

A LIFETIME OF ENJOYING YOUR CHILD

I hope that over the course of this book and your child's first years, you have discovered the joy of a child who has been nurtured by responsive parenting and who has been stimulated in ways that have made her happier and smarter. Your child's brain is far from fully developed. In fact, researchers and MRI studies now tell us that teenagers' brains are not yet fully developed and that this may account for some of the behaviors that are peculiar to teens and incomprehensible to adults. And though I've got a while before I'm parenting teenagers, I plan to continue to find ways to positively affect and enhance my children's potential.

New discoveries in neuroscience are always being made.

The study of the human brain is a fascinating topic, and what we'll learn next isn't clear. What we do know is that your brain continues to change over your lifetime. Providing the right kind of stimulation from the start of your baby's life can make her happier and smarter and will affect her in the most positive ways for the rest of her life.

appendix

Recommended Reading
and Resources

In this chapter, I've listed books, magazine articles, studies, and websites that I have found helpful and may be of interest to you. Please note that while website addresses are up-to-date as of publication of this book, they are subject to change.

Research in the area of brain development is ongoing, new theories are constantly being tested and reviewed, and new studies may appear. The same is true in the field of early childhood development.

When seeking answers to any of your questions about infants and development, you can find experts and advice on any subject. If you want to have a smarter, happier baby, my advice to you is the same, no matter what resources you utilize: know your baby, trust your instincts, and give your baby the right kind of stimulation.

Books

FROM BIRTH TO TODDLER, GENERAL INFORMATION

Your Baby and Child from Birth to Age Five by Penelope Leach (Alfred A. Knopf, N.Y.)

What to Expect When You're Expecting by Arlene Eisenberg, Heidi E. Murkoff, and Sandee E. Hathaway, B.S.N. (Workman Publishing, N.Y.)

What to Expect: The Toddler Years by Arlene Eisenberg, Heidi E. Murkoff, and Sandee E. Hathaway, B.S.N. (Workman Publishing, N.Y.)

Pregnancy, Childbirth and the Newborn: The Complete Guide by Penny Simkin, P.T.; Janet Whalley, R.N., B.S.N.; and Ann Keppler, R.N., M.N. (Meadowbrook Press, N.Y.)

Dr. Spock's Baby and Child Care by Benjamin Spock, M.D. and Michael B. Rothenberg, M.D. (Pocket Books, N.Y.)

Secrets of the Baby Whisperer by Tracy Hogg with Melinda Blau (Ballantine Books, N.Y.)

The Baby Book: Everything You Need to Know about Your Baby from Birth to Age Two by William Sears, M.D.; Martha Sears, R.N.; with James Sears, M.D. and Robert Sears, M.D. (Little Brown, N.Y.)

READING

Great Books for Babies and Toddlers by Kathleen Odean (Ballantine Books, N.Y.)

How to Get Your Child to Love Reading by Esmé Raji Codell (Algonquin Books of Chapel Hill, N.C.)

SIGN LANGUAGE

Baby Signs: How to Talk with Your Baby Before Your Baby Can Talk by Linda Acredolo, Ph.D. and Susan Goodwyn, Ph.D. with Doug Abrams (McGraw-Hill, N.Y.)

Baby Signs Series by Linda Acredolo, Ph.D. and Susan Goodwyn, Ph.D. (Board Book series that includes First Signs, Mealtimes, Bedtimes, Animals) (Harper Festival, N.Y.)

Baby Fingers: Teaching Your Baby to Sign by Lora Heller (Sterling Publishing, N.Y.)

Baby Sign Language Basics by Monta Z. Briant (Hay House, Inc., Carlsbad, Calif.)

Baby's First Signs by Kim Votry and Curt Waller (Gallaudet University Press, Washington, D.C.)

SLEEP

Healthy Sleep Habits, Happy Child by Marc Weissbluth, M.D. (Ballantine Books, N.Y.)

The No-Cry Sleep Solution by Elizabeth Pantley (McGraw-Hill, N.Y.)

Solve Your Child's Sleep Problems by Richard Ferber, M.D. (Simon & Schuster, N.Y.)

SOCIAL, EMOTIONAL, AND MENTAL DEVELOPMENT

Building Healthy Minds: The Six Experiences that Create Intelligence and Emotional Growth in Babies and Young Children by Stanley Greenspan, M.D. with Nancy Breslau Lewis (Perseus Publishing, N.Y.)

Touchpoints: Your Child's Emotional and Behavioral Development: The Essential Reference by T. Berry Brazelton (HarperCollins, N.Y.)

What's Going on in There? How the Brain and Mind Develop in the First Five Years of Life by Lise Eliot (Bantam Books, N.Y.)

Baby Mind: Brain-Building Games Your Baby Will Love by Linda Acredolo, Ph.D. and Susan Goodwyn, Ph.D. (Bantam Books, N.Y.)

Magic Trees of the Mind: How to Nurture Your Child's Intelligence, Creativity and Healthy Emotions from Birth Through Adolescence by Marian Diamond and Janet L. Hopson (Penguin USA, N.Y.)

Websites

There is a seemingly endless number of websites devoted to infant and child development. Following is a list of sites that I have found helpful as a parent. This list is not meant to be extensive but to provide you with some of the best-known parenting resources on the Web. Once you've started searching for information on these sites, it's easy to keep linking to new sites and discovering fresh information.

American Academy of Pediatrics: www.aap.org

BabyCenter: www.babycenter.com

Baby Prodigy: www.babyprodigy.com

How Kids Develop: www.howkidsdevelop.com

National Association for the Education of Young Children: www.naeyc.org

National Institute of Mental Health: www.nimh.nih.gov

New Horizons for Learning: www.newhorizons.org
Parents' Place at iVillage: www.parenting.ivillage.com
PBS Parents: www.pbs.org/parents/
Scholastic: www.scholastic.com/earlylearner/
The Children's Center: www.thechildrenscenter.org
The Parents' Press: www.parentspress.com
Zero to Three: www.zerotothree.org

Articles and Studies

Most of these articles and studies are easily accessed on-line. Websites are listed when available.

"Brain Development in Children." Dakota County, MN Social Services Department. Newsletter, July 2004.
    online at: www.co.dakota.mn.us/child_care/news_july. htm

"Building Your Child's Brain" from Tips To Grow By, Akron Children's Hospital, Akron, O.H.
    online at: www.akronchildrens.org/tips/pdfs/IN235.pdf

"Building Your Child's Brain." *Inside Children's,* a Publication of Akron Children's Hospital, Akron, OH. Summer 2002.
    online at: www.akronchildrens.org/elements/PDF/ InsideC-SprSum02.pdf

"Development in the First Years of Life." Ross A. Thompson. *The Future of Children,* Volume 11, Number 1. From *The Future of Children,* a publication of the David and Lucile Packard Foundation.
    online at: www.futureofchildren.org

"Fertile Minds." J. Madeleine Nash. *Time* magazine, February 3, 1997, Vol. 149, No. 5.

online at: www.thesmartbaby.com/timemagazinereport. htm

"In Focus: Understanding the Effects of Maltreatment on Early Brain Development." National Clearinghouse on Child Abuse and Neglect Information, Washington, D.C., October 2001.

online at: http://nccanch.acf.hhs.gov/pubs/focus/earlybrain.cfm

"What Research on the Brain Tells Us about Our Youngest Children." The White House Conference on Early Childhood Development and Learning, Washington, D.C. April 17, 1997.

online at: www.childrenslearning.com/linksandfiles

"Your Child's Brain." Sharon Begeley. *Newsweek,* February 19, 1996, pp. 55–61.

"Your Child's Brain: The Crucial First Years." Kathy Oliver. HGY 5318-98, Ohio State University Extension Factsheet, Family and Consumer Sciences, Columbus, O.H.

online at: http://ohioline.osu.edu/hyg-fact/5000/5318.html

Index

About the Author

$\mathcal{B}$efore having her first child in 1999, Barbara worked in the entertainment business, helping to produce comedy, drama, variety shows, and children's television. She is a graduate of the State University of New York at Albany and holds a degree in sociology. In 2001, while raising her first child as a "stay-at-home mom," with the help of her husband, Richard, she founded the Baby Prodigy Company. Barbara and Richard reside in Southern California with their two daughters, Samantha and Lara.

About the Type

This book was set in Caslon, a typeface first designed in 1722 by William Caslon. Its widespread use by most English printers in the early eighteenth century soon supplanted the Dutch typefaces that had formerly prevailed. The roman is considered a "workhorse" typeface due to its pleasant, open appearance, while the italic is exceedingly decorative.